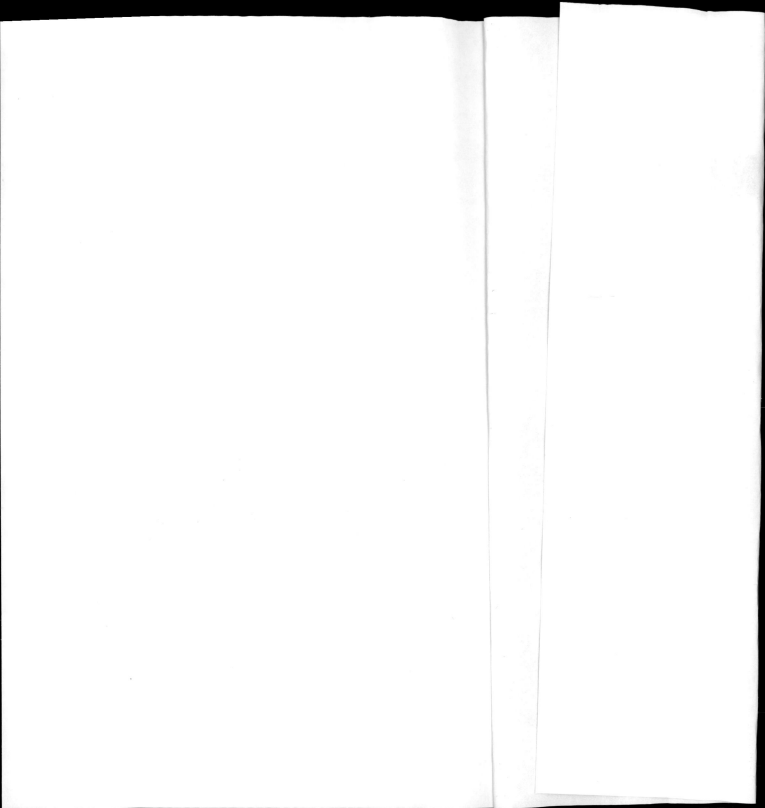

BAG MAN

★ THE ★
WILD CRIMES,
AUDACIOUS COVER-UP &
SPECTACULAR DOWNFALL
OF A BRAZEN CROOK IN THE
WHITE HOUSE

★ ★ ★ ★ ★

RACHEL MADDOW &
MICHAEL YARVITZ

CROWN
NEW YORK

Published in the United States by Crown, an imprint of Random House, a division of Penguin Random House LLC, New York.

CROWN and the Crown colophon are registered trademarks of Penguin Random House LLC.

Hardback ISBN 978-0-593-13668-3
Ebook ISBN 978-0-593-13669-0

Printed in the United States of America on acid-free paper

crownpublishing.com

2 4 6 8 9 7 5 3 1

First Edition

Chapter-opener art by Tom Bachtell

Book design by Elizabeth Rendfleisch

To the librarians and archivists who saved all this stuff.
God bless you and keep you.

"There is a mysticism about men. There is a quiet confidence. You look a man in the eye and you know he's got it. This guy has got it. If he doesn't, Nixon has made a bum choice."

—RICHARD NIXON, ON SELECTING SPIRO T. AGNEW
TO BE HIS VICE PRESIDENTIAL RUNNING MATE,
AUGUST 1968

★ ★ ★

CONTENTS

BAG MAN

"WHAT'S A SPIRO AGNEW?"

When Lyndon Johnson requested airtime one evening at the end of March 1968, network television bosses in the know assumed the president planned to address the nation on the growing conflict in Vietnam. LBJ certainly had some explaining to do on that front. He had campaigned for the presidency four years earlier on a pledge to keep America from getting dragged into a full-on war in Vietnam. He had promised that he would not send thousands of young American men "to do what Asian boys ought to be doing for themselves," that is, fighting off the Communists. But then he had done just what he said he would not.

By the time the 1968 presidential primary season was in full cry, with Johnson fighting off challenges from the peace-monger candidates in his own party, the war in Southeast Asia was not only raging but escalating. Dozens of U.S. soldiers and marines died every single day in Vietnam: every day, seven days a week. By that spring, many of the American boys being killed over there were draftees, not volunteers. The Tet Offensive, launched by the North Vietnamese forces at the end of January 1968, had spiked U.S. casualties on the battlefield. And spiked the number of troops Johnson said he needed on the ground in Vietnam. *More than half a million.* And all of that spiked doubt and frustration back home. After the surprise of Tet, the war suddenly seemed far from winnable anytime soon. More than a thousand American boys were dying every month, and nobody was sure this dear and bloody sacrifice would achieve anything worth having.

Johnson's nationally televised address on March 31, in prime time, unfurled—at the start—about as expected. While many Americans doubtless fumed about missing the new episode of *Bonanza* or *The Smothers Brothers Comedy Hour*, the president spent nearly three-quarters of an hour defending the war in Vietnam and restating its purpose. He granted the "pain [the war] has inflicted" and "the misgivings that it has aroused," but would not apologize for doing what he thought best. "What we are doing now, in Vietnam," he said, "is vital not only to the security of Southeast Asia, but it is vital to the security of every American." He was aiming for peace, and soon, he explained, but refused to give away the store to the Commies. "Our common resolve is unshakable," the president asserted, "and our common strength is invincible." He insisted that the enemy's recent campaign of attack was a failure. "[The Tet Offensive] did not collapse the elected government of South Vietnam or shatter its army—as the Communists had hoped," he said. "It did not produce a 'general uprising' among the people of the cities as they had predicted." But you could almost hear it in his hangdog voice; Johnson's own confidence seemed shaky.

And then, right at the end of his address, the president said something unthinkable, something nobody saw coming. "With America's sons in the fields far away, with America's future under challenge right here at home, with our hopes and the world's hopes for peace in the balance every day," he said, "I do not believe that I should devote an hour or a day of my time to any personal partisan causes or to any duties other than the awesome duties of the office—the Presidency of your country. Accordingly, I shall not seek, and I will not accept, the nomination of my party for another term as your President."

I shall not seek, and I will not accept. Good God.

A sitting president of the United States, constitutionally eligible to run for another term, decided—without warning to even his closest aides, without confiding completely in his own vice president—to call it quits.

That bombshell tossed into the middle of the presidential nominating process sent both Democrats and Republicans scrambling to recalculate their odds and their strategy. Each major party's nominating process had been a pretty wild political slalom that year. But now, with the incumbent's stunning announcement that he was leaving of his own accord and the race for the White House suddenly wide open, both the Democrats and the Republicans eventually decided to settle on tried-and-true figures for the top lines of their respective tickets: LBJ's incumbent vice president, Hubert Humphrey, would run for the Dems, and Eisenhower's old VP, Richard Nixon, would be the man for the Repubs. The only surprise on either slate turned out to be the man whom Nixon picked to be his running mate: a little-known first-term governor from a mid-Atlantic border state—a novice and novel political figure who would ultimately turn out to have far more impact on our national trajectory than most Americans have ever stopped to consider. His now-all-but-forgotten story has also turned out to be an odd historical doppelgänger, almost a premonition, for what the country would go through with the next Republican president who would face impeachment, after Nixon.

On paper, the Democrats' 1968 nominee—Humphrey—was a stolid, predictable, no-nonsense choice. Not only was he a household name for his long service as LBJ's vice president, but he had been a lion of the Senate, a brave and early champion of civil rights. A safe choice for the Dems. You might think. The optics of the Democrats' 1968 convention were considerably less reassuring. There were fits of pandemonium on the floor of the convention hall in

Chicago, led by antiwar Democratic delegates who were sure that Humphrey was poised to continue the grinding, disastrous war that was ripping the country apart.

And the action inside the hall was nothing compared with the energetic and riotous activity that all but shut down the streets surrounding the site of the convention, Chicago's International Amphitheater. Those frantic scenes became the enduring images of the 1968 presidential election: outrage and antiwar protests laced with paroxysms of violence; Mayor Richard Daley's Chicago police, joined by National Guardsmen, clubbing the "agitators" first into submission and then into paddy wagons.

A young Republican political operative sent to monitor the Democratic convention surveyed the scene and reported back on his findings. "We should side with Daley and the cops," twenty-nine-year-old Patrick Buchanan told his boss, the party's newly minted presidential nominee, who really didn't need to be told. Law and order, that was his thing.

The Republicans had held their own convention a thousand miles south of Chicago, in sunny Miami Beach, Florida, a few weeks earlier. And while the action inside the hall made it appear, at least to those watching at home, to be a considerably more genteel affair, the goings-on outside were something akin to the chaos that would soon unfold in Chicago.

Just as Republicans from across the country were in the midst of coronating Richard Nixon as their nominee, a torrent of violence and unrest was erupting just across town, in one of Miami's predominantly African American neighborhoods. What began as a "Vote Power" rally organized by local black leaders quickly turned into a violent confrontation with police.

Miami's malignantly bigoted police chief, Walter Headley—who had famously proclaimed a year earlier that "when the looting starts, the shooting starts"—confidently assured the public that his officers "know what to do." Hundreds of Miami city police, county police, and, eventually, National Guardsmen met the protesters with a show of force that included armored military vehicles, bayonets, and "clouds of tear gas." When all was said and done, three people were dead. And dozens more were injured, including a five-month-old baby who was teargassed by police. The officer responsible said of the incident, "I'd do it again." Though he added, "I'm sorry the baby got gassed."

Inside the protected confines of the Miami Beach Convention Center, it was lawful and orderly, with about as much drama as a gathering in Mamie Eisenhower's drawing room. Which was exactly what the Republican poohbahs were hoping for. They needed their party to be the real safe choice in these roiling times.

The GOP had kicked around the idea of nominating for president the moderate, aristocratic governor of New York, Nelson Rockefeller. Or maybe the Michigan governor, George Romney. There was a late flurry of interest in a comely new California governor named Ronald Reagan. Reagan had Barry Goldwater's hard-right politics, presented with a polish and sheen burnished on Hollywood's back lots. But Reagan was a novice. He'd run his first political race just two years earlier. Republicans instead settled on their own safer bet—a man with a big résumé, a reputation for political genius, and the tenacity of a rat terrier.

Richard Milhous Nixon was already, by then, a very familiar face in American politics. He was elected first to Congress in 1946, then to the Senate just four years later. He had been Dwight Eisenhower's vice president for two full terms, eight years dutifully serving at the shoulder of the most popular Republican president of the century to that point. Nixon had come within a whisker of the presidency himself in 1960, losing to John F. Kennedy in a race that was defined by Nixon flop-sweating his way through a debate with the slightly younger and much more telegenic senator from Massachusetts.

But even after that loss in 1960, even after an even more humiliating defeat in the race for governor in his home state of California two years later (even after he told the reporters who covered him, "Just think how much you're going to be missing. You don't have Nixon to kick around anymore"), he still refused to quit. He campaigned for Republicans across the country in the off-year election of 1966, earning due credit for helping Republicans rack up big gains in the House. And, cashing in those chits in the race for his party's presidential nomination, he handily dispatched all his rivals in 1968. He started as the front-runner, won almost every primary contest, easily batted down weak attempted challenges from Rockefeller on the left and Reagan on the right, and then won the nomination easily, on the first ballot of the convention in Miami.

Whatever else there is to be said about Richard Nixon, he was one hell of a political gamesman. Nixon understood that if he was to avoid losing the presidency—*again*—in what was sure to be another close race, he needed a number two on the ticket who added value, who shored him up where he was weakest. And so, the real business of the Miami Republican convention didn't happen on the floor, or even out in the streets beyond the convention hall. The real business of the convention happened in Richard Nixon's head and heart as he calculated his choice of a running mate.

There was plenty of buzz on the convention floor about the next veep nominee, on both sides of the party's political wings. The short list drawn up by the delegates and the network commentariat included that conservative up-and-comer from California, Ronald Reagan, as well as the moderate John Lindsay, the mayor of New York City. Nixon was reportedly agonizing over his pick; the press pack stalked the convention, in the sweltering August heat of Miami, hunting for word on the only real news to be had. Nixon pushed the decision later and later, until he finally made up his mind at the very last minute, on the last day of the convention.

At just before 12:30 that afternoon, with the hungry reporters duly alerted and assembled, Nixon finally emerged with the news they had been after. But first he teased, for drama's sake. "Our deliberations took place, for your information, throughout the night last night, except for one hour. I took that hour off for sleep," Nixon said. "They began again this morning at 9 o'clock and have continued until the present time." Then, finally, mercifully, Nixon came out with it. "I have now made a decision. I shall recommend to the convention that it nominate for vice president on the Republican ticket Governor Agnew of Maryland."

Governor Who? Of Where?

Even Governor Spiro Agnew himself was a bit taken aback, the way Nixon later told it. When a reporter on the convention floor asked how his running mate had reacted when he got the call, Nixon responded with glee and a rare flicker of humor. "I think the best indication of surprise is when a lawyer has no words," he said. "Governor Agnew, as you know, is a lawyer and is a very articulate man. . . . I'd say there's about 20 seconds before he said a word!"

In a year of boldfaced political names like Lyndon Johnson, Hubert Humphrey, Bobby Kennedy, Ed Muskie, Nelson Rockefeller, and Richard Nixon, this newcomer just didn't seem to fit the bill. Who the heck was Spiro Agnew?

Or, as the joke went at the time, "*What's* a Spiro Agnew?"

The country, like most of the working press, could be forgiven its ignorance. Spiro Agnew, aged forty-nine, had been governor of Maryland only eighteen months, having won office largely because the competing Democratic machines in Baltimore accidentally blew up their own party's primary and let the nomination go to a kook perennial candidate segregationist who publicly accepted the no-longer-quite-so-coveted endorsement of the Ku Klux Klan.

Agnew's gubernatorial victory certainly didn't owe to his long history in Maryland state politics. He had won exactly *one* race in his entire career to that point, serving as county executive, which is sort of like being mayor of Baltimore County, from 1962 to 1966. So of course nobody outside Maryland knew much about him. Really, nobody inside Maryland knew much about him. Spiro Agnew had gone from obscure local official, to fluke governor of Maryland, to the nominee for the vice presidency of the United States in less than six years.

The choice was a genuine surprise to everyone: to Agnew, to the Republican Party, to the national political press corps, to the rest of his fellow Americans, most of whom were just learning his name. And then puzzling out why exactly a guy with a Greek name was an Episcopalian.

The Nixon team, however, knew exactly who (and what) Spiro Agnew was, even without taking the time to learn much about him and even without bothering to vet him too awfully closely. For Nixon and his team, Spiro Agnew represented political expediency. What looked to outsiders like a roll of the dice, a dangerous gamble, was actually a result of Nixon's reading the political landscape from thirty thousand feet. Humphrey would be tough enough to beat on his own, and Nixon was already worried about a third-party challenge from the populist, racist former Alabama governor George Wallace—a potential shot to the heart of the Republicans' emerging southern strategy. Nixon had seen enough of Agnew to know he could help where it counted most.

Governor Spiro Agnew of Maryland

Dueling narratives about the new vice presidential nominee emerged before the Republicans even broke camp in Miami. The GOP message gurus introduced Spiro T. Agnew—"Ted" to his friends—as a political figure best captured by the catchy radio jingle created when he ran for Maryland governor just a few years earlier, sung to the tune of Frank Sinatra's "My Kind of Town (Chicago Is)":

"My kind of man, Ted Agnew is!

"My kind of man, Ted Agnew is! Our great new talent for! Governor! And what's more, he's your kind of man, Ted Agnew is! Taking your stand, Ted Agnew is!"

In the Republican telling, Agnew was a blue-collar, tell-it-like-it-is leader who could appeal to working-class voters because he was one of them. He was not a career politician but the son of Greek immigrants who put himself through law school after honorably serving the country in the military (including earning a Bronze Star for his service during the Battle of the Bulge). He was a political outsider, a straight shooter defined by straight-up American ideals: hard work, honesty, integrity. Agnew was that kind of man. "Well, I like him because he's honest," one supporter offered, "he's really honest."

The Dems wasted no time in constructing a Spiro Agnew counter-narrative, releasing their own TV ad highlighting Agnew's complete lack of experience on the national stage. It was, well, kind of mean-spirited when you get right down to it. The spot begins with a tight and inelegantly framed shot of a small corner of a television set, with its ungainly fat channel-changing knob as the focus. Then comes the sound of a man, off camera but apparently tuned in to the set, beginning to chuckle. The camera slowly pulls out as the man's laughter grows louder and more insistent, to the point of hysteria, until the lettering on the television is revealed in full: "Agnew for Vice-President?" The laughing fit continues after a hard cut to the next screen, white lettering on a black background: "This would be funny if it weren't so serious." As the 1968 general election season got under way, the Democrats seemed intent on having sport with Spiro Agnew. They were going to make him a laughingstock. A national joke.

But a funny thing happened on the way to the White House that year. The Dems soon found out Spiro Agnew could give as good as he got. They learned that if you wanted to play nasty, Spiro Agnew was all in. He was blunt. He was vociferously politically incorrect. He was likely to answer any opposition jabs with a flurry of roundhouses and haymakers. And that made his campaign events a sensation the national news media could not ignore.

Agnew could be counted on to taunt antiwar protesters, East Coast "elites," and the unwashed "hippies" who, in his telling, contributed nothing useful to society. "I'll tell you this," Agnew said at a rally in York, Pennsylvania, "they can't run a bus, they can't serve in a governmental office, they can't run a lathe in a factory, all they can do is lay down in the park and sleep or kick policemen with razor blades!"

"Somewhere, somebody failed you," Agnew barked at a group of hecklers, while the cameras rolled. "Your churches must not have gotten through to you because you don't even know anything about the golden rule! . . . I'm frankly ashamed of you. And I think you ought to be ashamed of yourselves."

The crowds who came out to his rallies reveled in Agnew's unapologetic take-the-paint-off-the-walls partisanship. His increasingly confrontational taunts became a constant presence on the network newscasts. What news executive could pass on scenes like this?

Governor Agnew's lack of filter occasionally led him into controversy on issues of race and ethnicity that might have shamed other pols. Like his law-and-order insistence that petty looters ought to be shot by police. Sure, the cops should try to make an arrest first, but if that fails, "the officer should not hesitate to shoot him." After the collective horror generated by that position, Agnew clarified that he just meant that taking aim at a few looters "would be a tremendous deterrent." During one short stretch of the campaign, he was forced to apologize for crudely referring to Polish American voters as "Polacks," and then immediately thereafter for describing a Japanese American newspaper reporter as a "Fat Jap." Agnew promised that he meant no offense with the remarks, apologizing, he said, "if I have inadvertently offended anyone." But close observers began to get the feeling there was nothing *inadvertent* about it. Reporters covering him on the trail at the time said he was undaunted by the criticism, apology notwithstanding. They started calling the incident "the boo-boo in a muu-muu."

Spiro Agnew's political brand was built around the idea that he was an outsider who had never been a card-carrying member of the patrician establishment. It would have been off message, off brand, for him to start acting like a career pol either—careful, measured, mealy. And if he didn't actually appear to care whom he had offended, that became a feature of his candidacy, not a bug. Rather than hurting him, his "slip-ups" seemed to solidify his support with the Republican base.

"I guess by nature I'm a counter-puncher," he proudly told reporters. "You can't hit my team in the groin and expect me to stand here and smile about it."

Agnew counterpunched himself all the way to the White House, at the side of Richard Nixon. And he didn't stop once he settled in behind his new desk on Pennsylvania Avenue. "In Spiro Agnew," wrote that young Nixon political op, Pat Buchanan, "I found a fighting ally in the White House, a man with guts and humor, willing to give back as good as he got, who did not flinch from battle. He relished it."

Funny thing this, old habits die hard. And when the

exercise of those habits has delivered fame and glory and raucous applause, they are unlikely to die at all. It is a rare man or woman who is ever really changed by ascension to high office, or tempered by the solemnity of the oaths they have sworn or by the national duties they have shouldered. And Spiro Agnew was certainly not among that rare breed.

Temperamentally, ethically, he was largely untouched by office. But the reverse is hardly true. Spiro Agnew left indelible marks on his office, on his party, on his government, and on his country.

And yet, for all his very real impact, Agnew's story is largely forgotten today. Even fairly assiduous students of America's modern political history can be forgiven for being a tad fuzzy on what exactly prompted Agnew's dramatic resignation from office in 1973. *It was some penny-ante tax evasion back in Maryland, right?*

Part of the reason for the lost history of Spiro Agnew is the simple factor of time. It's been more than fifty years since that 1968 campaign season, and nearly fifty since he resigned the vice presidency in disgrace. But time alone does not account for Agnew's obscurity. Agnew's downfall, of course, was also overwhelmed by the sheer epic sprawling disaster of Richard Nixon and the Watergate scandal—the only scandal in living memory to unseat a president.

But it's definitely worth stopping and considering Spiro Agnew and his crimes and misdeeds all on their own. Because Agnew's is a story of a scandal so brazen that, had it not occurred at the same time as Watergate, would likely be remembered as the most astonishing and sordid chapter visited upon a White House in modern times. Heck, in any times.

Agnew's is a tale of a thoroughly corrupt occupant of the White House whose crimes are discovered by his own Justice Department and who then clings to high office by using the power and prerogative of that same office to save himself.

And the playbook Agnew wrote to try to save himself has left its own long legacy. For the elected official who prides himself on busting through political norms—and insists on always punching back harder than hit—it's a pretty straightforward set of plays. And leaves no time to fret over the destruction you leave behind. If saving yourself means undermining the institutions of democracy—the Department of Justice and the free press, for starters—well, fire up the backhoe. Obstruct the investigations of your crimes; smear and threaten and demand investigations of the investigators; play the victim; indict the press; throw up a smoke screen of legal argument, no matter how bizarre or foundationless. *The vice president of the United States cannot be indicted while in office. Says so in the Constitution. Sort of.* And by all means convince your legion of supporters that the allegations against you are all vicious lies, that the evidence against you is conjured and concocted by enemies threatened by your overwhelming political strength. That it's all just a big witch hunt.

But there is another piece of the Agnew story also worth considering, one with a slightly happier tincture. Because the whole story of Agnew's crimes and his downfall and his descent, ultimately, into something between ignominy and obscurity is not all bad, or entirely dispiriting. This is also the story of faceless but faithful public servants doing their jobs with thoroughgoing integrity. It's the story of determined young federal prosecutors who uncovered the crimes of a politician at the very top, faced down a torrent of threats to their persons and to their investigation, and refused to stop until the truth emerged. It's also the story of their bosses at the Department of Justice who shielded them from the predations of Agnew and his partisans.

Terrible people doing terrible things is a (terrible) fact of life, but it doesn't ordinarily bring on a constitutional crisis; it's the reason we have law enforcement. But when the very worst people are at the top of American government, and willing to use the awesome powers of their office to stay there and thwart justice, the protection of the Constitution requires the very *best* people, also in office, willing to stand up and do what's right. This is that story, too.

And if any of this sounds familiar, it's because history really is here to help.

CHAPTER 1

★ ★ ★

DIVIDER IN CHIEF

*N*BC *interrupts its regular program schedule to bring you the following special report."*

The urgent, static-filled announcement cut into NBC's prime-time lineup on the evening of April 4, 1968, just four days after President Johnson's dramatic withdrawal from the race for the presidency.

The election was still seven months away. Richard Nixon had not yet secured the Republican nomination, and Spiro Agnew had only just passed the one-year mark of his undistinguished and unremarkable term as governor of Maryland. He was an afterthought or, more precisely, a non-thought in national Republican politics. But the bulletin of April 4, and the days that followed, began to change all that.

It was a Thursday evening, in the heart of prime time, when NBC News broke into its regular programming. "Martin Luther King Junior was killed tonight in Memphis, Tennessee," the newsman Chet Huntley somberly reported, "shot in the face as he stood alone on the balcony of his hotel room. He died in a hospital an hour later."

The Reverend Dr. Martin Luther King Jr. had been in Memphis in support of African American sanitation workers striking in protest of insufficient pay and unsafe working conditions, marching with signs that read, I AM A MAN. Dr. King's murder sent waves of shock, panic, fear, and anger rippling through the country.

The Democratic presidential candidate Bobby Kennedy— whose own brother had met the same fate four and a half years earlier, and who himself would be brought down by an assassin's bullet months later—delivered the news to a stunned, mostly African American crowd on the streets of Indianapolis. "Martin Luther King dedicated his life to love and to justice between fellow human beings," Kennedy said. He recognized the understandable human responses of "bitterness, and hatred and a desire for revenge" in the face of this injustice and pain. But he begged for understanding and calm, in keeping with King's lessons of nonviolence. "I shall ask you tonight to return home to say a prayer for the family of Martin Luther King," Kennedy implored, "but importantly to say a prayer for our own country."

Indianapolis did remain calm. But as the news of the assassination spread late that night and early into the next morning, parts of America were convulsed by shock, and outrage, and, in a handful of cities, full-fledged riots. One of those cities was Baltimore. In that critical moment, with so much hanging in delicate balance, Maryland's new Republican governor, Spiro T. Agnew, decided to respond to the crisis in his state's largest city with brute force. And with political posturing that would make a peacock blush.

Agnew ordered more than five thousand Maryland National Guard troops onto Baltimore's streets, armed with live ammunition. Those troops joined a force of twelve hundred city police officers and an additional four hundred state troopers who had already been dispatched to the riot areas. The soldiers and police systematically swept the city, arresting thousands of residents involved, or suspected to be involved, in the riots.

When nearly seven thousand National Guardsmen and police officers weren't enough to quell the unrest, Agnew declared that an "insurrection" was under way in his state. This permitted him to make a formal request to President Johnson, asking for an additional two thousand active-duty U.S. Army soldiers to join the Guardsmen. The arrival of soldiers from the Eighteenth Airborne Corps Artillery marked the first time federal troops had been deployed in Baltimore since just after the Civil War. U.S.

military jeeps with barbed wire across their hoods rolled through city streets, while Governor Agnew presided over the law-and-order response from the state capital.

Six days into the crisis—with more than five thousand protesters jailed, six people dead, and Baltimore still aflame—Agnew finally reached out to somebody other than law enforcement and the military. The governor called a select group of African American community leaders to a meeting at a state government building in downtown Baltimore. Black Baltimore had voted over-whelmingly for Agnew against his Klan-endorsed, nutball Dixiecrat opponent, so they represented a real bloc of the governor's voting base. Which meant most of these men and women had reason to expect a frank and respectful discussion about how best to join with law enforcement to help calm the violence. What they got at the meeting—which was televised live at the governor's invitation—was something altogether different.

Agnew filibustered from the start, wagging his finger at the assembled black leaders, laying the blame for the vio-lence at their feet, lecturing them about how they had failed to stand up to the younger and more militant black champions, whom Agnew called "the circuit riding . . . caterwauling, riot-inciting, burn-America-down type of leader." The group understood pretty quickly that Agnew had invited them to this meeting for one simple reason: they were props in his scripted and televised set piece.

More than half of the community leaders walked out in protest during Agnew's screed. "He is as sick as any bigot in America," one pastor said on his way out. "He is as sick as anything I have seen in America."

Letters and calls to the governor protesting his high-handed and disrespectful treatment of the African American community in Maryland were swamped by letters and calls in support of Agnew's performance. Among those in support was Richard Nixon's brash, young, white-nationalist speechwriter, Pat Buchanan. "Agnew had called in these civil rights leaders and asked, 'Why aren't you condemning the violence?'" Buchanan later said. "And the objection a lot of people made was he brought in TV cameras and read them the riot act." Agnew had pulled off the kind of twofer Buchanan appreciated. The governor had come down hard on the uprising in his state, and he had created his own made-for-television moment to publicly browbeat his opposition. This guy knew how to use television, and without breaking a sweat. Buchanan immediately sent Agnew's speech to Nixon, "and he was very impressed by [Agnew's] toughness."

Agnew's specific brand of "toughness" appealed to Nixon at that moment in particular because he was already anticipating a snag in his election plans—a snag named George Wallace. The unreconstructed segregationist and recent governor of Alabama had thrown his hat in the ring as an independent candidate for president, which made for a perilous new challenge from the far-right flank. Nixon was counting on overwhelming support from conservative whites in the Deep South to defeat the Democrat Hubert Humphrey that November, but if George Wallace managed to peel off enough of that vote, he might starve the Republican ticket of enough support to cost Nixon the White House. By another maddeningly slim margin. Again.

And so what Nixon and Pat Buchanan saw in Agnew that April in Baltimore looked like an answer to their electoral map problems by August. "His toughness would help us in the border states," Buchanan said of Agnew. "If we're running against Wallace, we're not going to win Alabama, Louisiana, Georgia, Mississippi. But Tennessee, Arkansas, Texas, Florida, the upper/outer South? We could win that."

Spiro Agnew was Richard Nixon's kind of man.

Nixon campaigned across the country that fall, while Spiro Agnew concentrated on those southern border states, delivering what Buchanan described as a "hardline" message. And while George Wallace did manage to pick off Deep South states like Alabama and Mississippi that November, the Nixon-Agnew ticket won Tennessee and Florida, and the Carolinas, and Virginia and Missouri and Kentucky. They held on and—in a squeaker—won the White House, beating Hubert Humphrey with a little more than 43 percent of the popular vote.

Richard Nixon's calculation worked. But what he got in his new vice president was something more than he bargained for, in a few different ways. Not the least of which was that Agnew was becoming a star in the making in the Republican Party, a politician whose appeal to the conservative base would quickly outstrip even Nixon's own.

Agnew on the campaign trail

★ ★ ★

IT'S NOT OFTEN that a *vice president* manages to command so much of the spotlight in the first years of a new presidency. And Spiro Agnew didn't even have to work that hard at it. From the moment he stepped into the White House, Agnew just did what he had been doing since he was tapped to be running mate—and since the riots in Baltimore.

Nixon was maybe a bit too educated, and too versed in the intricacies of governance and policy, which meant he came across as wonky at times, or overarticulate, which translated to most of the voting public as inarticulate. Agnew was like Nixon's id—without the burden of much actual knowledge or curiosity or responsibility to the country at large. He was a heat-seeking political missile who embraced the power of television and the value of a well-landed attack, low blow or not.

If anything, Vice President Agnew got *more* aggressive over time. His default setting was attack mode. He cheerfully derided liberals, the establishment, ivory-tower professors, and the press. It wasn't that he was proselytizing for his own cause or for pet policy ideas; instead, he made a marquee act out of just taking a flamethrower to the other side. Which itself effectively became Agnew's cause. At least it became his mission as vice president. Why sermonize about the superiority of your ideas and values when it was so much more effective to attack the motives and character of your opponents, to call them names, to question their love of country. The vice presidency of Spiro T. Agnew marked the birth of the bruising, know-nothing confrontational conservatism that has been eating the lunch of seemly, Kiwanis Club Republicanism ever since.

So while Nixon worked to find accommodation with Democrats on policy issues in Washington, Agnew flew around the country to antagonize and belittle those same members of Congress. "You know how it is with the radical liberals," he opined to one crowd in Connecticut, "you zing one of them—call his hand, cite his voting record, quote his speeches, tell America the harm he's done—and he howls like a coyote with his tail caught in a snake hole!" The response was rapturous applause.

During one post-election stop in Springfield, Illinois, Agnew played to a raucous crowd by railing against weak-kneed liberals whose un-American character "translates into a whimpering isolationism in foreign policy, a mulish obstructionism in domestic policy, and a pusillani-

mous pussyfooting on the critical issue of law and order!"
He dismissed critics of the Nixon administration as "nattering nabobs of negativism." He joked that they had
formed their own 4-H Club, "the hopeless, hysterical hypochondriacs of history." He even coined a phrase for the
nation-threatening lefties: "radic-libs," short for "radical
liberals."

Hell, Agnew seemed to love the partisan political work
assigned him as vice president—especially now that he
had the benefit of some excellent White House–grade staff
work. Some of his best lines were written by Buchanan and
William Safire, the young wordsmiths who specialized in
derisive appellation. "Nattering nabobs of negativism" was
the brainchild of Safire. Buchanan penned "pusillanimous
pussyfooters." But Agnew wanted it known that he, too,
was pretty good at an insult. "An effete corps of impudent
snobs who characterize themselves as intellectuals"—that
was all me, Spiro would say. "Agnew told me years ago that
he had come up with it himself," reported another former
speechwriter, "and Safire subsequently confirmed it."

If the emerging public image of Agnew was as a singu-
larly divisive national figure, he embraced it. "He was
asked why he—more than other politicians—was accused
of dividing the country," NBC's David Brinkley reported in
1971. "Agnew said it was because he was the foremost de-
stroyer of liberal dogma, and that when liberals are attacked, they salivate like Pavlovian dogs."

Republican partisans loved him, and the bolder the better. "They saw somebody who they thought they could rely
on, they thought they could trust, they thought they could

like, and so they were attracted to him," says one of Agnew's top White House aides, David Keene. "The way he said things was sort of refreshingly courageous."

"Enthusiasm for Agnew's knock-heads maledictions against the protesters, the youth marchers, the TV commentators, the New York *Times,* the Washington *Post, et al* has swept through Middle America like the croup," *Life* magazine noted in 1970. "If, in the process, he is maybe further polarizing the country, widening the rift with the young'uns, at least the oldsters are finding in him a great source of solace."

"He said what a lot of us have always suspected," said one Nebraska Republican official, "and we're glad to have it confirmed as so."

It wasn't just among his supporters that Agnew was having a very real effect. The vice president's unflagging and unapologetic partisanship drove his antagonists, well, a tad bonkers. After the vice president publicly attacked the nation's black leaders for blaming the rest of society for their own community's ills, one of the most prominent African American members of Congress—Representative William Clay of Missouri—took to the floor of the House to deliver a condemnation that can still make your eyes water, even today.

"[He] is seriously ill," Clay began. "He has all the symptoms of an intellectual misfit. His recent tirade . . . is just part of a game played by him called mental masturbation. Apparently, Mr. Agnew is an intellectual sadist who experiences intellectual orgasms by attacking, humiliating, and kicking the oppressed."

Intellectual orgasms? The man could inspire, that's for sure.

A confidential source informed the FBI in October 1970 that a group known as the East Side Crazies had drawn up a detailed plan to assassinate Agnew on his next visit to New York City. "There are a lot of people around here who would like to blow the [obscenity] up," one female member had reportedly bragged. The group even had "numerous places where bombs and ammo are stored" on the city's East Side, the informant reported, to be used in such an attack. (The FBI was concerned enough to pass along the tip to the Secret Service.)

There were other, more creative plots targeting Agnew, including one involving an antiwar activist who worked backstage as a page on ABC's Sunday public affairs show *Issues and Answers*. The young peacenik was tasked with preparing the drinks of choice for the show's guests. And when Spiro Agnew was booked as a guest one Sunday, the page, John Henry Browne, saw the perfect chance to take some measure of revenge on the vice president. "I'd brought a tab of LSD to the studio," Browne later wrote, long after he had become a famed defense attorney. "It was in my pants pocket. As I slowly prepared Agnew's Manhattan, I awaited my chance.

"The national audience would see the man undergo a psychotic breakdown. I didn't care. . . . Agnew deserved it."

In the end, Browne couldn't pull the trippy trigger; he left the tab of LSD in his pocket, sparing Vice President Agnew a television appearance for the ages and likely sparing himself some prison time.

★ ★ ★

THAT SAID, THE prospect of Agnew experiencing an acid trip live on the set of a national *news* program might have felt like karma to some, because the group that he reserved the most venom for, his favorite target of all, was the press.

In his first year in office, the vice president set himself to the task of what he believed was justified revenge on the fourth estate. The negative press he had received as a candidate, he told David Keene, was due not to his numerous gaffes but to biased news reporters who had turned on him once he joined the Republican ticket. "He said, 'You know, I was governor of Maryland. According to *The Washington Post,* I was the brightest governor in the East, I was this wonderful guy. And then, one night, Richard Nixon picks me as his running mate, and the next morning I'm the dumbest son of a bitch ever born.' He said, 'Now, they might have gotten it wrong the first time, but I didn't change that much overnight.'"

The White House was a pretty nice platform to use for evening the score. And Agnew had the blessing of President Nixon, who was himself nursing some pretty significant and growing resentments against the press. When Agnew let it be known he wanted to take Buchanan's advice to use his appearance at the Midwest Regional Republican meeting in Des Moines to attack the national press—and specifically the big three network news organizations—Nixon was all in. Buchanan took the proposed speech over to the president for his review. Nixon read it carefully, pen in hand, ready to make emendations.

"As he quietly read," Buchanan later wrote, "I heard Nixon mutter, 'This'll tear the scabs off those bastards.'"

In a series of speeches at the end of 1969, with the seal of the vice presidency on every lectern and podium, Agnew delivered scabrous attacks on the major news networks and the "little group of men" who ran them. The way he told it, he pitted average Americans against the "elite" newsmen in New York and Washington who, he ominously noted, "wield a free hand in selecting, presenting, and interpreting the great issues in our nation."

What Joe McCarthy had done to try to stir up fear and suspicion in the general public about the Commies in the 1950s, Agnew was effectively trying to replicate a decade and a half later when it came to members of the press.

"What do Americans know of the men who wield this power?" Agnew asked during a nationally televised speech from Des Moines. "Of the men who produce and direct the network news, the nation knows practically nothing. Of the commentators, most Americans know little other than that they reflect an urbane and assured presence, seemingly well-informed on every important matter."

These newsmen, Agnew asserted, were subtly injecting their own bias into each report: "A raised eyebrow, an inflection of the voice, a caustic remark dropped in the middle of a broadcast can raise doubts in a million minds about the veracity of a public official or the wisdom of a government policy."

Presidents and vice presidents had, of course, tangled with the press before, but Agnew didn't stick to the old playbook of disputing specific facts or arguing specific reports. He was going one step further. At a time when tens of millions of Americans got their news from the big three television networks—NBC's newscast alone had twenty million viewers each night—Spiro Agnew was sowing distrust in the judgment and patriotism and credibility of all news executives and anchors and correspondents. *Who elected them?* He was attacking the institution of the free press itself.

Republicans in Congress rushed to Agnew's side. "I think the networks deserve a thorough goosing," said the party leader in the Senate, Hugh Scott. "We have truth in advertising and truth in labeling. I think television might experiment with some straight news."

The Republican senator Paul Fannin of Arizona cheered Agnew's remarks as well, saying, "The plain fact is the vice president has applied the prod to a sacred cow and the bellowing is being heard across the land." The political power of the media that Agnew was drawing attention to, Senator George Murphy of California added, "could become the greatest danger to the future of our democratic system of government."

The vice president, emboldened, also began to make what the networks viewed as not-so-veiled threats of government censorship. Agnew reminded Americans that the federal government "licensed" television airwaves and that it was—to put a fine point on it—"a matter of immense importance to the American public that information flow credibly and freely to them." Seemingly following Agnew's lead, the Nixon administration's FCC chairman took the extraordinary step of requesting the transcripts of Vietnam commentaries aired on the three major news networks.

The president of NBC News appeared on the nightly newscast to push back. "Evidently, he would prefer a different kind of television reporting," he said of Agnew, "one that would be subservient to whatever political group happens to be in authority at the time. Those who might feel momentary agreement with his remarks should think carefully about whether that kind of television news is what they want."

The president of the American Society of Newspaper Editors went a step further, saying that Agnew's speeches against the press were an attempt to bring newspapers and broadcasters "under some form of covert control," as in Russia.

The suggestion, also voiced by Democrats in Congress, that Agnew's attacks were creeping dangerously close to some form of Soviet-style authoritarianism had little effect. Agnew refused to back down. Nixon and Agnew, they were the real victims here. "I'm not out to vilify or attack anybody," Agnew told a crowd in Alabama, "but I think if this country is going to remain great, it's extremely important that the people who are in positions of leadership are not intimidated by the news media, and I don't intend to be intimidated!"

The Washington Post was among the many news outlets to identify a particularly perfidious by-product of Agnew's repeated targeting of East Coast newsmen. "One little noted and wholly unintentional result of Vice President

Agnew's speeches against the press and television," the *Post* reported, "is a renewed wave of public expression of anti-Semitism. It was noticeable at once in this city where local television stations were swamped for three days after Agnew's first speech with obscene phone calls protesting 'Jew-Commies on the air.'"

Agnew was not directly espousing anti-Semitic beliefs, but his dog-whistle references to the hidden hand of a "little group of men" in New York and Washington emboldened a segment of his base already inclined toward such views. A Jewish newspaper editor in Louisville, Kentucky, reported he had been "buried under an avalanche of sick [anti-Semitic] mail" in the wake of Agnew's speeches. A leading Jewish organization warned at the time that extremist groups across the country appeared to be "using Agnew's speeches to justify their hate campaigns and urging their followers to support him."

The way Agnew saw it, any backlash against him was overblown and manufactured, more unhinged ranting from those "hopeless, hysterical hypochondriacs of history." This was just Agnew being Agnew. "I've always lived by my instincts," he once said. "If people are telling me 25 good reasons for doing A, and yet there's still a feeling I have that I should do B, I go with my feeling. . . . It's a subliminal type of intelligence."

And what was Agnew's reward for this reliance on his own gut instinct and his own subliminal intelligence? How about a second term! How about a Nixon-Agnew victory in the 1972 election that was in actual fact a political annihilation of the radic-libs and their standard-bearer,

George McGovern? The Republican incumbents in 1972 won forty-nine states, won the electoral college 520 to 17, and won the popular vote by nearly twenty million votes, 61 percent to 37 percent.

Spiro Agnew (*right*) and his wife,
Judy (*second from right*)

January 20, 1973, was a warm and balmy evening in Washington, D.C., a beautiful night to celebrate an inauguration, the kind of weather that portended all good things for the future. Among other things worth celebrating: Spiro Agnew, the now-second-term vice president, was the apparent front-runner for the 1976 Republican presidential nomination. Agnew and his wife, Judy, were feted that night at a party the Smithsonian threw in their honor. Judy Agnew appeared both ecstatic and relieved. She told NBC's Barbara Walters that the festivities were a little easier than the first time around, four years earlier, because "this time, I know more or less what to expect!"

As Walters asked Judy what she did expect, Agnew quickly interjected on his wife's behalf, "She expects to have fun!"

CHAPTER 2

★ ★ ★

FOLLOW THE MONEY

When the sound of a single shotgun blast ruptured the quiet dawn of a beautiful spring morning on the Eastern Shore of Maryland, the caretaker of Mulberry Hill Farm was pretty sure it came from inside the property's stables. He rushed to the horse barn that morning, May 24, 1973, and discovered a man lying face up, with a gaping wound in his chest and a shotgun at his side. The caretaker knew the man on sight. The victim had boarded his horses at Mulberry Farm for years and made regular early morning visits to the stables. And he was no ordinary citizen, but the U.S. congressman for Maryland's First District, William Oswald Mills. Mills was in the middle of his first full term, a former telephone company executive who was, by all accounts, a likable guy. He was an Elk *and* a Rotarian. Only forty-eight years old, Mills was already possessed of a reassuring grandfatherly countenance. He had a round, friendly face and big, slightly goofy, black-rimmed glasses.

What had happened to him that late May morning was no great mystery. A note found at the scene was among seven Mills left behind. "I've done nothing wrong, but there's no way I can prove it," read one. "This is the only way out." The State's Attorney told reporters that the gunshot wound appeared to be "self-inflicted."

Congressman Mills was not a well-known political figure outside his home district, but news of his death spread across the country. A newspaper in California went with this headline: "First Watergate Suicide."

Watergate was a slow-developing scandal. The actual break-ins at the Democratic National Committee headquarters at the Watergate office complex had taken place about a year earlier, when the 1972 general election campaign was just getting under way. The burglars were caught red-handed on their final attempt, and it took only a matter of days for newspaper reporters and the FBI to tie the five Watergate burglary perps—and the cash they were carrying—to Nixon's Committee to Re-elect the President (the unfortunately named CREEP) and to one of the presi-

dent's key political advisers. But it wasn't until the following spring that investigators began to follow a trail of
misdeeds right into the Oval Office. And President Nixon
embarked on ever more frantic efforts to sweep away the
bread crumbs that led to his own door.

On the last day of April 1973, Nixon was already sweep-
ing hard, scapegoating his closest aides in the White
House, H. R. Haldeman, John Ehrlichman, and John
Dean. He went on live television to tell the nation he was
accepting "full responsibility" for the questionable actions
of these subordinates. Which was his way of saying that
the questionable actions were his subordinates', and not
his own. And yes, Haldeman, Ehrlichman, and Dean were
all losing their prized White House sinecures. But the fact
that the president had cleaned house, had removed the
malefactors, did not altogether satisfy. "This rotten vine of
Watergate has produced poisonous fruit," said the Senate
Republican leader, Hugh Scott, "and all nourished by it
should be cast out of the Garden of Eden."

A month later, there were two full-on investigations
under way. Nixon's own attorney general had sworn in the
former solicitor general Archibald Cox as the special prosecutor in charge of the Department of Justice's probe into
the Watergate burglary and the possible cover-up that followed. Cox told reporters he had been given, and he promised to exercise, the authority to follow the facts wherever
they led. "Whatever else I shall be," he said, "I shall be independent." The Senate Watergate Committee, meanwhile, had begun its hearings, which meant that an endless
stream of fascinating, obscure personalities and subplots

were all beginning to play out like a soap opera on national television every afternoon.

Among the unexpected walk-on characters in the first week of the Senate hearings had been Congressman Mills from Maryland. It was in connection not with the actual break-in at the Watergate complex but with the political group behind it: the Committee to Re-elect the President, which was suspected of being the source of "hush money" payments made to the Watergate burglars. Amid efforts to account for that group's profligate and questionable spending, Representative William Mills's name popped up.

Records showed the Mills congressional campaign was the recipient of a mysterious infusion of cash from CREEP: $25,000. The payment was arranged through Nixon's then campaign manager, John Mitchell (who would later be sent to prison), and though it was a relatively small amount of money, the contribution, for some reason, was never reported. Mills insisted to reporters that he had done nothing wrong. He claimed that it was just an innocent accounting oversight by his campaign.

But then, four days after the revelation about the phantom $25,000, the congressman was dead, by his own hand. Watergate was no lark, no empty exercise. While it was unfolding, no one knew where it would end, or whom it would expose. For the country at large, it was an ever-growing, slowly building political spectacle. But for people caught in its web, it must have been terrifying.

The Watergate-era suicide of Congressman William Mills also brought together two seemingly disparate law enforcement story lines: the riveting national scandal of Watergate, and the long-simmering *non*-scandal of everyday corruption and bribery in the home state of both Mills and Spiro Agnew. In Maryland, in the early 1970s, unexplained campaign contributions and questionable accounting practices —that was politics on a good day.

Notorious dens of political corruption like New Jersey and Illinois captured the national headlines in the 1960s and 1970s, but it was Maryland's politicians who were being marched off to federal prison at a steady and pretty impressive clip: a sitting U.S. senator from Maryland indicted on ten separate counts of soliciting and receiving bribes while in office (the charges were later reduced); a two-term U.S. congressman sent to federal prison after pocketing cash bribes from local banks; a former Speaker of Maryland's House of Delegates sentenced to three years for his involvement in a savings and loan scheme.

Corruption in Maryland was not just expected; it was so yawn-inducingly common that when one county official was convicted for taking bribes and sentenced to eighteen months behind bars, his constituents threw him a going-away party. And more than a thousand of them showed up to cheer their man! *Hooray for you! See you when you get out! We'll hold your seat for ya!*

So in 1973, while the rest of the country might have been in the grip of "Watergate fever," a handful of young federal prosecutors working out of the U.S. Attorney's office in Baltimore—Tim Baker, Ron Liebman, and Barney Skolnik—were fishing closer to home, trawling for evidence of good old-fashioned Maryland corruption. "In essence it was follow the money," says Liebman. "Get the documents, follow the money."

Inside or outside Washington, if the Watergate era had a theme song, this was it. The FBI and congressional investigators and intrepid reporters from *The Washington Post* and even a special prosecutor were all busy "following the money" in the burglary and the vast cover-up that reached deep into Richard Nixon's inner circle. All over the country, prosecutors seemed, well, inspired by the times. By October 1972, the U.S. Attorney in Baltimore, working *sotto voce* with a team of local IRS agents, had developed enough leads into financial irregularities in Baltimore County to warrant assigning three young prosecutors to a corruption case there, full-time. "Investigate!" Barney Skolnik, the senior prosecutor on the team, says they were told. "Which is like throwing catnip. 'Okay, fine! We'll investigate!'"

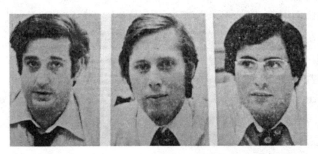

From left: Assistant U.S. Attorneys Barney Skolnik,
Tim Baker, and Ron Liebman

Skolnik, at the ripe old age of thirty-two, was at the time already perhaps the most feared federal prosecutor in the state of Maryland. A gruff New Yorker—with the accent to prove it—he had already sent to prison a handful of crooked county officials and businessmen and, most impressively, *two* members of Congress. One of Skolnik's quarry suggested the young prosecutor was making the state look bad. Maryland didn't necessarily have worse corruption than other states, he insisted: "The difference between Maryland and other places is Skolnik. If you put that man in another state, he'd do exactly the same thing. I've never seen a man with such drive."

If Skolnik was the grizzled veteran on the team, with a belt full of notches to prove it, Ron Liebman was the noob. He was twenty-nine years old and brand-new to the U.S. Attorney's office, having just arrived from a tour with the "other side."

Tall and lanky with a big bushy head of hair, Liebman had been working as an apprentice for one of the most sought-after criminal defense attorneys in Maryland, a legendary lawyer named Arnold Weiner. Weiner had often defended the allegedly corrupt Maryland political characters whom Skolnik was going after, and Liebman had sometimes watched from Weiner's second chair. By the time Liebman decided to become a prosecutor, the young lawyer was familiar with the general odor of Maryland politics, having once defended a local businessman accused of bribing an elected official with, among other things, a John Deere tractor.

Tim Baker, the third member of the team, was the one with the gold-plated pedigree. Son of a wealthy Maryland real estate developer, Baker was a graduate of Harvard

Law School; he had been a member of the prestigious *Law Review* there, and then won a coveted Supreme Court clerkship with Chief Justice Warren Burger. He was thirty years old.

The three young prosecutors complemented one another: Skolnik the experienced and irascible leader, Liebman the rookie who had taken a peek behind the curtain on the other side, and the book-smart Baker, who quickly fell into the role of de facto "chief of staff," keeping the team organized and on task.

And the team pretty immediately got results. Within three months of getting the assignment to go after Baltimore County corruption, the three had gained authorization from a federal grand jury to blanket the county with more than two dozen subpoenas.

The wave of court orders was set to go out on January 4, 1973, just two weeks before Nixon and Agnew were to be inaugurated for their second term. Not that the Baltimore prosecutors were much concerned about that, except insofar as it meant they had the assurance that their boss, who had been appointed by Nixon, would likely be around for a good long while.

That was good, because the prosecutors expected to need some time to develop their case. The IRS agents they were working with were tasked with uncovering instances of engineering and architectural firms in Baltimore County withdrawing huge sums of cash from their bank accounts, which was a big tell. "Rule one," a veteran federal prosecutor had counseled the Baltimore team, "look for pools of cash. . . . Cash is the medium for corruption." As they considered their potential targets for criminal charges, the key questions for the prosecutors were these: How much of this cash from the engineering and architectural firms was finding its way into pockets of local elected officials who awarded construction contracts, and who exactly were those officials? For Skolnik, Liebman, and Baker, step one was that boatload of subpoenas, which were addressed to the firms that had received the highest number of contracts from the county—plus one subpoena earmarked for the Baltimore County government itself.

On the appointed day, a team of specialized IRS agents fanned out across Baltimore County to hand deliver the document demands to the companies at the center of the investigation. The prosecutors served all the subpoenas at once, with no warning. They hoped to unsettle their marks. "When you serve these subpoenas, if you can serve it at a guy's home rather than the office, do it," Ron Liebman recalls telling the agents. "And if you can do it in the evening in between his martini and dinner, fine." Two overzealous and literal-minded agents took those instructions too much to heart, bursting into the home of one executive during dinner and terrifying the man whose cooperation they would ultimately need. "That you can't do!" Liebman told the agents. "That's Gestapo tactics." The federal prosecutors did mean to unsettle, but not to terrorize. There's that delicate balance again.

The idea was to "try and give the tree as big a shake as we could," Baker remembers, and see what would fall out.

The shaking part succeeded, judging from the blaring headline in *The Baltimore Sun* the next morning: "Subpoenas Catch Baltimore County Off Guard."

The legal papers, delivered to twenty-six separate private firms, demanded years of records related to county contracts. The subpoena served to the county government itself demanded a vast trove of documents the prosecutors suspected would reveal how public works contracts had really been awarded. There were also going to be invitations to appear at the federal grand jury already impaneled in downtown Baltimore.

"They'd never experienced a federal grand jury investigation before," Baker says, "let alone having [dozens of] grand jury subpoenas dropped on them within a matter of an hour."

One slightly stunned Baltimore County official, William Fornoff, complained to the *Sun* about the amount of documents the prosecutors were asking for. "It's going to be a helluva big bunch of records" they would need to get together, Fornoff complained to the reporter. "Just the stacks of cancelled checks for the two-year period [alone]," he estimated, "would form a wall 5 feet high and 15 feet long."

The prosecutors didn't much care; they wanted all of it. Notes, minutes of meetings, everything the county had on its process for awarding contracts. The information was eventually loaded onto a truck and dropped on the doorstep of the U.S. Attorney's office, where IRS agents were eagerly waiting.

A "war room" had been set up in a fourth-floor office at

the federal courthouse. The small room quickly overflowed with files and stacks of papers—years of county records and boxes of canceled checks from the businesses—as IRS agents bent themselves to the painstaking and picayune task of sifting through every jot and tittle in the paper trail. "They would just go through them, hundreds and hundreds and hundreds of checks," Baker says. "But they knew what they were looking for."

The IRS team was looking for something very specific in the financial documents: suspicious-looking transactions with no obvious on-the-books application. They flagged things like frequent "bonuses" paid out to company executives, which was a good way to generate cash to pay bribes. Where that loose cash ended up would be harder to trace. "The general thinking was maybe we'd be able to find a corrupt congressman, maybe a state legislator," remembers Ron Liebman.

Dale Anderson

If this was a bit of a fishing expedition in the early stages, the prosecutors hooked a big fish, fast: the sitting Baltimore County executive at the time, a Democrat named N. Dale Anderson. Anderson had held that position for six years, and although the job title sounds more middle manager than man in charge, being Baltimore County executive made Dale Anderson one of the most powerful Democrats in the entire state. The prosecutors had heard some unsavory whispers about the way Anderson conducted county business.

"The word on the street," says Barney Skolnik, "the rumor, the scuttlebutt, is that Dale Anderson is corrupt and is taking bribes."

Anderson's alleged racket was that he demanded cash kickbacks from contractors for the county projects he controlled, things like road and bridge engineering contracts. A kickback is the kind of move you learn on day one of gangster and corruption school: *I make sure you get the contract, you then pay me (cash, please) a portion of what that contract is going to pay you. You win, I win, the taxpayers can suck it.* In Anderson's case, the kickback scheme was not only widely discussed; it wasn't even much of a scandal. At least he wasn't doing much to hide it. Ander-

William Fornoff

son's wife, the prosecutors heard, had regularly been paying the couple's mortgage at the bank in crisp $100 bills.

As the three prosecutors and the IRS agents began digging into the documents at hand, they discovered that the scuttlebutt about Dale Anderson was considerably more than talk. They quickly generated hard evidence that Anderson was, in fact, pocketing cash payoffs from the architects and engineers to whom he was awarding big-dollar contracts for county projects.

That stunned-seeming county official, William Fornoff—

the one who complained to the newspaper about how *difficult* it was going to be to produce the records the prosecutors wanted—was, it turned out, in on the whole thing, too. "The game," says Skolnik, "was you put cash in white envelopes and you give it to Fornoff. And Fornoff was the only one who actually handed the cash to Dale Anderson."

That made Fornoff the "bag man": the buffer between the architects and engineers paying the cash kickbacks and the politician receiving them. It was textbook bribery and corruption. And the Baltimore prosecutors were just starting to peel back the layers of it. They figured Anderson and Fornoff couldn't be the only malefactors. And, like the Watergate special prosecutor Archibald Cox, they were determined to follow the facts, to follow the money, wherever it might lead.

CHAPTER 3

★ ★ ★

JUST BEING CAREFUL

Federal prosecutors have bosses, and while those bosses are expected to be independent arbiters of justice, they are also political animals, appointed by elected officials and usually along party lines. The U.S. Attorney in Baltimore was no different. George Beall, still in his early thirties, had a boyish face that made him look even younger than he was and a perfectly coiffed head of dirty-blond hair. He was clean-cut, handsome, and very much a known quantity in the world of Maryland politics. A graduate of Princeton University and the University of Virginia Law School, Beall had made himself a dependable cog in the state's Republican machine—a member of the party's central committee and a recipient of political appointments from Republican administrations.

More than that, though, George Beall was something akin to Republican royalty in the state of Maryland. His father had been a long-serving U.S. senator, and his oldest brother, Glenn, had been elected to the U.S. House of Representatives before moving on to the Senate, regaining for the family (and for the GOP) the seat his father had lost to an upstart Democrat. The Beall family Republican pedigree seemed the best explanation for why, in the spring of 1970, Richard Nixon had picked the thirty-two-year-old neophyte prosecutor to be the U.S. Attorney for the District of Maryland.

His relative youth notwithstanding, nobody questioned Beall's good sense or his motives, even when, less than two years into his stint as U.S. Attorney, he made

U.S. Attorney George Beall

the decision to prioritize the pervasive and embarrassing problem of political corruption in his home state.

The investigative work began, rather inconspicuously, with a letter Beall wrote to the commissioner of the IRS in

March 1972. "In the past this office has received allegations which suggest that there have been violations of the
criminal tax laws in Baltimore County," the letter read,
"some of which appear to involve local political corruption." Beall was planning a grand jury probe into the rumors and would welcome some IRS manpower for the
effort. There was reason to believe that the criminality
went well beyond just tax evasion, but Beall made a decision to put IRS personnel on the front lines of the investigation, rather than FBI agents, because the feebs tended to
leave big red flags in their wake. Beall preferred to keep
this investigation under the radar at first. Why make people nervous?

But the evidence turned out to be so flagrant it threatened to speak for itself. The volley of surprise subpoenas
sent out just before inauguration day in January 1973
pretty immediately started to reveal signs of possible
bribes being paid for government contracts—the evidence
that first implicated Baltimore County's sitting chief executive, Dale Anderson.

If Anderson was corrupt and taking bribes, Beall and
his prosecutors thought, perhaps they could nail a few
other county-level officials as well. This seemed likely to be
a pretty noteworthy prosecutorial haul, but hardly earth-
shattering; what the IRS agents and the trio of young prosecutors under Beall were halfway already to proving was
basically garden-variety Maryland political corruption, in
this case by old-guard Democrats. So it was kind of a surprise when Beall got a phone call about the newly developing case early one afternoon in February 1973. A call from

Richard Kleindienst. The attorney general. Of the United States. Especially because Beall hadn't yet *informed* the AG about the investigation. And why would he? The U.S. Attorney's office in Baltimore had a proud legacy of independence, and no one on the case thought the attorney general needed—or even wanted—to be clued in to the early stages of a middling corruption investigation involving local pols.

"If you're investigating a county executive, particularly a Democrat, it wouldn't even occur to you to tell the department," says Tim Baker. "None of their business! . . . As far as [Beall] was concerned, there was nothing to report."

Beall took the unexpected call from Attorney General Kleindienst that February afternoon. And then he gathered Skolnik, Liebman, and Baker to give them a readout: "Kleindienst was basically calling to say, 'What's going on here?!'"

The reason Kleindienst was pressing, Beall reported to his prosecutors, was that he had just had an encounter— that morning—with someone who seemed "very nervous" about the investigation in Baltimore County. That someone was the vice president of the United States. Vice President Agnew had gotten word that federal officials were poking around in his old neck of the woods, so he went right to the top—Agnew was never a subtle man—and grilled the attorney general, over breakfast, for answers about an investigation that Kleindienst hadn't even known existed.

Beall told his team that he had assured the attorney general that they were only looking into local public officials. Their investigation had nothing at all to do with Vice

President Agnew. As Beall talked, though, Tim Baker's an-
tennae went up. The vice president had served a four-year
term as Baltimore County executive before moving up to
the governor's mansion. He was the man who had held
Dale Anderson's job before he did—the *very last man* to
hold the exact job the prosecutors were now discovering
was a hive of corruption. Agnew's immediate successor
was under federal investigation for taking bribes in a well-
feathered kickback system that did not appear to be particularly, um, innovative.

The attorney general reaching out, on behalf of the vice
president, to the chief federal prosecutor in Maryland—
the prosecutor appointed by Richard Nixon—seemed
more than suspicious to Tim Baker; it seemed like a flash-
ing red light. "I immediately thought to myself, 'Why is
[the vice president] so upset?' He's upset because he's got
something to hide!" Baker remembers.

"We're going to get Agnew!" Baker blurted out to the rest
of the group. He was sure of it.

His fellow prosecutors waved him off. "I remember
thinking, 'So the vice president [talked to] the attorney
general,'" says Liebman. "He'd been governor, he'd been in
county government, maybe he was just being careful."

"[We] had a consciousness that [Agnew] was the predecessor," Skolnik remembers. But the prosecution team
also knew that Spiro Agnew was, legally speaking, off-
limits. Not because he was the sitting vice president, but
because the statute of limitations had run out on anything
that Agnew had possibly done while county executive. It
had been more than six years since Agnew ran Baltimore

County. Even if he had done something wrong back then—and that was still a big "if"—enough years had passed that he was now safe from prosecution. So long as he had been clean *since* then. Which, of course, he had to be, right? How on God's green earth could a national figure, a man second in line to the most powerful office on the planet, a sitting vice president of the United States of America, be so dumb, or so venal, to still be pocketing bribes? It couldn't be.

★ ★ ★

LESTER MATZ KNEW he was on the prosecutors' radar in the spring of 1973, and he was plenty nervous about it. He really, really, really didn't want to have to tell them all he knew or all he had done.

Matz and his partner, John Childs, ran a local engineering company that had been scooping up valuable contracts from the Baltimore County government for years. By some estimates, Matz, Childs & Associates received more than twice the county contracts as any other similar firm.

Business was booming right up to the moment the IRS agents came knocking with one of their subpoenas in January 1973. The physical subpoena was followed up by a personal phone call from the prosecutor Tim Baker, who didn't exactly beat around the bush. "I want to advise you in a formal way that you're in a lot of trouble," Baker said. "What I think you should do is to get yourself a lawyer, a criminal lawyer, and have him get in touch with me as soon as possible."

Lester Matz

Turned out to be good advice. It was only a matter of weeks after the subpoenas were served on Matz, Childs & Associates before its lower-level executives were summoned for questioning about a very specific oddity in the company's books. IRS agents had turned up a pattern of suspicious "bonus" checks, issued to executives, who were then withdrawing that supposed bonus money from the bank in crisp $100 bills. The prosecutors suspected this was a scheme to generate the cash to pay bribes. And once you suspected it and knew where to look, the money was pretty easy to follow. Yes, on the company's books, the payments were just supposed to look like compensation to select employees. But the employees wouldn't actually get to keep the money; they'd deposit the bonus checks in their own bank accounts, keep a small amount to cover the taxes on the purported "bonus," withdraw the rest in cash, and then give the cash back to the company. It was simple money laundering, using the personal bank accounts of their own employees as the Laundromat. Sometimes the employees did get to pocket a little sliver of the money to keep them happy enough (and quiet enough) about the whole rigamarole, but the bottom line was that the company ended up with the un-booked cash. The question was why. To find out, the prosecutors needed people at the company to tell them who was ending up with all those crisp hundreds.

One by one, Tim Baker summoned the executives from Lester Matz's firm for questioning in front of the federal grand jury. "We'd show them the checks," he recalls, "and then say, 'You got X hundred dollars. You withdrew nineteen $100 bills. What'd you do with them?'"

What Baker and his fellow prosecutors got in return, over and over, was nada. "You get a lot of 'I don't know. I can't remember. I can't remember,'" says Ron Liebman.

They would remind the witnesses that failing to recall a key fact was fine, as long as the prosecutors didn't learn later that they were actively trying to cover up something. "If you *do* remember," Liebman would tell them, "and we find out that you *should* have remembered and should have answered that question, you'll be very unhappy." Sitting in federal prison unhappy. But the witnesses continued to bob and weave, avoiding straight answers.

Barney Skolnik had no patience for non-answers. When it came to recalcitrant witnesses, Liebman says, Skolnik was "an absolute master"—especially when tangling with those who had convenient losses of memory in the grand jury room. "If he was questioning a witness," Liebman says, "and that witness had a fact in his head, Barney was going to get that fact out. Without question." He did it in the fashion of Columbo, the disheveled and shuffling TV cop of the time, the detective who always managed to herd the stray facts into the pen by episode's end.

While Liebman and Baker furiously pressed a witness for some piece of information, only to come up empty, the physically unassuming Skolnik sat back and watched. "Barney would come in late," Liebman says. "He looked like he just got out of bed. He's kind of tired, maybe he'd shaved in the morning, maybe he didn't. And he'd sit there with a Styrofoam cup of coffee, to all intents and purposes appearing not to even be paying attention."

And then, Liebman remembers, suddenly Skolnik "would put his hand on my arm, raise his finger, and say, 'Can I take it from here?' And it was incredible. I mean, the kind of lawyering, the kind of not only brilliance but the ability to interrogate someone who is holding on for dear life to something that's terribly incriminating and get it out every time, was incredible."

Sometimes, as Skolnik closed in on some suspicious "bonus" check or some other detail, a witness would make a grab for the magic get-out-of-jail-free card: his Fifth Amendment rights. *I will respectfully decline to answer that question on the grounds that it might incriminate me.* The young federal prosecutors were ready for that, too, in a Swiss Army knife sort of way. They were armed with an all-in-one carrot-*and*-stick response. And they had it courtesy of Richard Nixon's law-and-order agenda—a dubious new provision in the Organized Crime Control Act of 1970 called "use immunity." (On the day the Senate passed that law, Nixon turned to his then attorney general, John Mitchell, and the then FBI director, J. Edgar Hoover, those twin paragons of justice, and said, "I give you the tools. You do the job.") Use immunity was like a trapdoor in the Fifth Amendment.

There was no need for the executives to fear incriminating themselves, the prosecutors explained to the witnesses in the Baltimore grand jury room, because the government was hereby granting them immunity to tell exactly what they knew. Their testimony could not be used as evidence against them in any prosecution, and so their Fifth Amendment right to avoid self-incrimination was protected. That was the carrot.

But those witnesses also thereby lost the ability to keep their mouths shut about any crime they were involved in that they didn't want to talk about. With the judge's okay, prosecutors effectively forced immunity onto their witnesses—whether they wanted it or not—compelling them to testify, or face the consequences.

"We had a court order that they had to testify," says Baker. "[The judge] would say, 'Look, you don't testify, I'll hold you in contempt. You can go across the street, spend a couple days in the Baltimore City Jail, see how you like that.' I mean, the Baltimore City Jail, in those days, was a dungeon."

That was the stick, and a good one, too.

"We started getting these guys to tell us what happened. They had expected to be in there for five minutes and leave, and instead they were in there for an hour, grilled, blabbing away!"

The witnesses eventually sketched the outlines of a textbook criminal bribery scheme and began to shade in the detail. A Matz, Childs employee would receive a "bonus" check, deposit it in the bank, withdraw the money in $100 bills, and pass it back to Lester Matz. Matz would then stuff it in an envelope and hand it over to Dale Anderson. Not to Dale directly, of course, but to County Administrator William Fornoff. The bag man.

With the banking records in hand, and grand jury testimony to explain the transactions and their purpose, Skolnik, Liebman, and Baker were building an airtight case not only against Fornoff and Anderson for extortion but also against Matz for paying the bribes. Prosecutors had solid evidence of at least five separate kickback payments totaling $5,000. And, the noose was tightening in May 1973. Word around Baltimore was that Fornoff was starting to talk to the prosecutors and might turn on his co-conspirators.

And then Lester Matz himself opened a line of communication with the prosecutors, through his lawyer Joe Kaplan. Tim Baker took a hard line with Kaplan. The government had overwhelming evidence against his client, and conviction at trial was pretty much a slam-dunk proposition. Matz was also a little late booking passage to safe ground. Baker told Kaplan he wanted him to persuade Matz to cop to the bribery scheme and cooperate with the prosecution. And do it fast. Matz would be much better served making a deal now than trying to fight a battle he couldn't win in court. Kaplan wouldn't agree. He kept telling the prosecutors that Matz and his partner, John Childs, had compelling reasons to keep quiet. And then he went one step further, hesitantly relaying to Baker that Matz and

Childs were "very concerned about the national implications of the information which they possess."

"[Kaplan] said something to Tim," recalls Ron Liebman, "to the effect that 'you don't want to know what you have here.'"

Baker kept up the pressure, but Kaplan remained frustratingly noncommittal. He said he wasn't sure Baker's higher-ups would even be "interested" in the type of information his clients had—an obvious reference to George Beall, who had, after all, been appointed to his job by a Republican president.

The entire U.S. Attorney's office, right to the top, "was interested in doing its job" no matter who was involved, Baker insisted. Kaplan remained maddeningly slippery on the subject of his client until the end of May, when Baker got the call he'd been waiting for: Kaplan was coming in for a serious talk.

"I have this vague recollection of him sitting in front of my desk," Baker says of that meeting with Kaplan, "and he's very nervous. . . . He says, 'This goes much farther than you realize.'"

The information Matz and his partner possessed "was sufficient to convict a high federal official of serious offenses," Kaplan told Baker, and his clients expected "full immunity" in exchange. Kaplan then provided the outlines of what Matz knew.

Skolnik, working right down the hall, didn't even know the meeting was on the schedule, until it was over. "Timmy Baker comes into my office and he closes the door, which is unusual," Skolnik says. Baker explained to his team leader that Kaplan "wants to bring Matz in, and Matz wants to be brought in, but there's a problem."

Baker hesitated for a beat. "What?! What?!" Skolnik interjected.

"Uhh, they paid off Agnew," Baker replied.

And it wasn't only back in the day, when Agnew was county executive. Matz, it seemed, had continued making the payoffs when Agnew became governor of Maryland and then right into his tenure in his latest government position. Agnew was still taking bribes? As vice president? In Washington? Now? Yes, yes, yes, and yes.

"Timmy was, like, peeing his pants," Barney Skolnik says. To Skolnik, the grizzled veteran, this unmasking of the sitting vice president seemed like "one of those things that can't be true because it's too good to be true. I mean cash in white envelopes? I mean, that's crazy."

If it did turn out to be true, which now seemed at least plausible, the three young prosecutors had just uncovered a case that would surely be the biggest of their lives, no matter how many more years they worked. This was high-stakes prosecutorial poker. If they pushed this against a sitting vice president and won, the three men and their boss could end up heroes. On the other hand, if they pushed it and failed, they could end up pariahs in the legal profession and in the country at large. "We realized at that moment," Liebman remembers, almost fifty years after the fact, "that we had a tiger by the tail."

CHAPTER 4

★ ★ ★

"OTHERWISE DECENT"

When Lester Matz finally came into the U.S. Attorney's office in Baltimore to tell his story to prosecutors, he started at the beginning. Matz and his partner, John Childs, had been in the engineering consulting business for more than two decades by then, and had built one of the most successful firms in the state of Maryland. But he was still nursing grievances from the early days, back in the 1950s, when he was shut out of the lucrative engineer-

ing and surveying contracts being handed out in Baltimore County. There were a handful of favored companies
who got all the engineering contracts. These favored firms
had long-standing relationships with the county officials
who awarded the contracts, and a big part of the relationship, it was understood, was a willingness to kick back a
percentage of the money in the contract to the county executive and his friends.

Matz's luck changed when a recent acquaintance,
Spiro T. Agnew, was elected Baltimore County's new executive in November 1962. Matz had made a sizable do-
nation to Agnew's campaign, and Agnew thought the
engineer could be even more help to him in office. The
newly elected county executive, Matz said, was already
clued in to the pay-for-play schemes that ruled the bidding
process for the county's public works contracts. But Agnew
apparently thought Matz could bring a patina of rational
professionalism to the process. Through an intermedi-
ary, Agnew asked Matz to draw up a game plan: a chart,
with real numbers, about how much engineers could reasonably be expected to pay on various sizes of contracts.
Engineer that he was, Matz ran the numbers, calculated
expected profit margins on different types of road, bridge,
and sewer projects, and filled in the chart. Agnew seemed
pleased with the results. Generally speaking, from a rational business point of view, the kickbacks would average
around 5 percent of the value of each contract.

This could mean real money, because when Agnew
took office in December 1962, Baltimore County, like suburban areas all over America, was in the clover and grow-

ing fast. The increase wasn't just folks from farm country heading closer to the cities, where the jobs were, as in the decades before World War II; in the years after the war, city dwellers were leaving urban areas for the sylvan dream of the suburban ranch house with a yard for the kids. The population spike in places like Baltimore County necessitated new roads and bridges and sewer lines and sewage treatment plants and police stations and firehouses and on and on. The growing tax base, and generous grants from federal and state governments, meant a lot of money was sloshing around in the system, controlled by the Baltimore County government, which was now run by Spiro T. Agnew.

Word got out pretty fast in the Agnew years: if you were an engineering firm hoping to land a big project from the Baltimore County government, you had to schmear Spiro. Not simply a handshake and a few hundred bucks, or a meager drive-by contribution to his next campaign. Even then, before he became a national figure, Agnew was no piker; he expected a kickback of 3 to 5 percent of the total value of county contracts (thank you, Lester Matz). And he wanted to make sure there was no traceable record of the payments. So he wanted them delivered by hand. In cash.

When he traded up to the governorship of Maryland on January 25, 1967, Agnew took the cash-in-an-envelope maneuver with him to Annapolis. As governor, of course, he would control much larger and more lucrative state contracts. Enormous contracts. When Matz sat down and did a back-of-the-envelope calculation on what he owed Agnew for the contracts he had won in Agnew's first year as governor, he was shocked by the total. But Matz was a man of his word, and 5 percent was the agreed-upon price. He felt honor bound to fulfill his "obligation" to the governor. And in July 1968, just a month before Nixon chose Agnew as his running mate, Matz set up a one-on-one meeting in the governor's office and delivered to Agnew an envelope stuffed with $20,000 in cash.

He personally handed Agnew the cash while "standing by the fireplace in Agnew's office in the State Office Building."

"At that point, he told Agnew what the money was for," Tim Baker wrote in his notes, "and the ensuing conversation was not about 'political contributions' but about the connection between the money and the [engineering] jobs."

Baker and his fellow prosecutors still remember Matz reluctantly recounting that story, full of shame, which fit a mold Skolnik, Liebman, and Baker were already well acquainted with: a lot of people agonized over choices they had made, or had been forced to make. "These were otherwise decent [businessmen]," Liebman says, "and it was killing them. They were doing it, but it bothered them. And once they started telling us these stories, we could see how really troubled they were."

But there it was. As county executive and then as governor of Maryland, Agnew conducted a full-on bribery racket, extorting businessmen across his state—and pocketing a fat cut of the funds appropriated for public works projects. Nobody doing business with the state was confused about the extracurriculars required to win a bid.

"All these business guys understood that if you're competent and you want your fair share of the work, you gotta pay," says Liebman. "If you don't pay, you don't get [the work]. It doesn't matter that you're the guy who can design the Chesapeake Bay Bridge better than anyone else. If you want that work, you've got to kick back."

But all this paled against Matz's other revelation: a remarkable fact, and the most potentially far-reaching one, something the attorney Kaplan had hinted at in his earlier meeting with Baker. The expectation of payment, according to Matz, did not end when Agnew left the governor's mansion for his next job, in the White House. Liebman still recalls in vivid detail a story Matz related: "After the election [in 1968], the vice president's temporary office was in the basement of the Old Executive Office Building. And Lester Matz went to see the vice president elect with an envelope stuffed with cash in his suit jacket pocket. He walked in to see Agnew—as he told us the story and as I recall it—and one of them, I think maybe Agnew, pointed to the ceiling like, 'Don't say anything because we could be overheard or taped or something.' And Matz took out this envelope with $10,000 in cash and handed it to Agnew. Agnew took it, put it in the center drawer of his desk, and closed his desk."

And Matz's visits did not stop once the vice president settled into his permanent office, right across from the White House on the second floor of the Old Executive Office Building.

Agnew instructed Matz to visit the White House anytime he had cash to deliver. All he had to do to get a meeting was call his secretary and tell her he had "information" for the vice president. So Lester Matz returned. Each time secretly handing the vice president of the United States envelopes stuffed with "information": $9,000 on one visit; $10,000 the next; and another $5,000 the next.

"I was shocked, just shocked. We all were," Liebman says.

"What stuck in my mind about it," adds Tim Baker, "was this was *in* the White House."

As it turned out, there was documentary evidence backing Matz's extraordinary claim—a record of the vice president's meetings inside his office on the White House grounds. The prosecutors were able to access the Secret Service logs of every visit to the vice president's office. What the prosecutors found in those logs corroborated Matz's statement: a trip by Matz to see the vice president

U.S. Secret Service appointment record for one of
Lester Matz's visits to Vice President Agnew
in April 1971

on March 18, 1969; a return on April 18; another just a week later, on April 24.

After one of these visits, Matz told the prosecutors, he returned home to Maryland shaken by what he had done. He solemnly confided in his partner, John Childs, that they had just paid off the vice president of the United States.

"I mean, taking large sums of cash in a succession of white envelopes—over and over and over again—is about as crass as it can be if you're a public official," says Barney Skolnik. "It doesn't even deserve the appellation 'scheme.' It wasn't a scheme; it was just a payoff."

The prosecutors turned up a similar arrangement Agnew had with a Maryland engineering company executive named Allen Green. Green had been handing cash to Agnew in return for state engineering contracts since early in his term as governor, after listening to Agnew cry poverty. Agnew had never made any real money before he assumed public office, he whined to Green. He didn't have an inheritance. His term as county executive had been a great financial sacrifice, because the salary was so paltry. The governor's salary was better, but hardly sufficient for Agnew to live in the style he felt his new public position demanded. Green understood, as the prosecutors noted, "he was being invited in a clear and subtle way to make payments."

The payments from Green continued after Agnew decamped for Washington, when Agnew had grown less subtle in his asks. Green was given to understand that an Agnew associate had drawn up a list of all the state contracts Green had been awarded in the previous two years, contracts that would continue to pay out. So starting at the end of 1968, and throughout the entire first term of the Nixon administration, Green told prosecutors, he made trips to Agnew's office three or four times a year, each time carrying $2,000. Always in envelopes. Always in cash. In all, Green paid Agnew a total of almost $30,000 in cash over his first term as vice president. Agnew would usually take the envelope and, without a word of acknowledgment, tuck it into his desk drawer or his coat pocket.

The White House logs confirmed Green's visits also: a trip to see Agnew on February 10, 1969, just a few weeks after the inauguration; another trip in July; another appointment that October. The entry for one visit noted that Green even "had [a] gift" when he arrived at the White House—an expensive new "Pulsar watch."

Green's deliveries weren't confined to the White House grounds. In 1969, when Agnew and Nixon were first sworn into office, vice presidents didn't get an official residence at the U.S. Naval Observatory as they do now. Free to live where he wanted, Spiro Agnew and his wife, Judy, chose to take up residence in a fancy suite at the Sheraton-Park Hotel. Inside that suite rented for the vice president by U.S. taxpayers, Agnew accepted more deliveries of cash. Green's payments had continued until just a few weeks before Agnew was sworn in for a second term.

The cash payoffs that Agnew was demanding from Green and Matz during his time in the White House were primarily for previous contracts he had awarded to them while he was Maryland governor, which continued to generate handsome profits for the engineers. Just because he had moved on to a higher office didn't mean he no longer deserved a taste of those profits, Agnew told them. But with his new office came new opportunities as well. And so, in addition to the old contracts Agnew had given out as governor, he quickly got to work on steering brand-new federal contracts to the businessmen who were now streaming into his office with those wads of cash.

With his eyes constantly on the prize, Agnew rankled the top Nixon aides H. R. Haldeman and John Ehrlichman by effectively trying to wrestle control of the federal contract-awarding process and centralize it inside his vice presidential office. The not exactly doe-eyed Ehrlichman was stunned after witnessing Agnew trying to grab control of plum federal government contracts by telling President Nixon that he was concerned "our friends" were being discriminated against when it came to how those lucrative contracts were being handed out.

Though Agnew failed in his larger effort to get all patronage contracts on the Eastern Seaboard cleared through him personally, his attempts were not entirely in vain. Agnew got word to Lester Matz, on at least one occasion, that a particular federal job up for grabs could be his for the princely sum of $2,500 cash in Agnew's pocket. Matz arranged for the job to go to a friend whose firm Matz had a financial stake in. He met the friend across the street from the White House, gathered up the required amount of cash, placed the envelope on the vice president's desk.

And magically, the job went to Matz's friend who had quietly bought and paid for it. It was the federal government, for sale.

These young public servants from Baltimore had not set out to find this level of corruption. But now they had turned up rock-solid evidence that the vice president of the United States was running an undercover bribery and extortion scheme from inside the White House. And their discovery had come at a particularly delicate moment in the nation's history—a moment when an entirely different, and much more public, scandal was first beginning to close in on President Nixon.

"Like everybody else in the country, we were fascinated and obsessed with what's going on with Watergate," Baker says, "and we could see how it related to us."

"The president of the United States, to put it mildly, is under a cloud," says Liebman, "and here we three Baltimore federal prosecutors are being told that the next guy in line, the guy a heartbeat away, he's also under a cloud!"

Says Baker, "We could certainly see the gravity."

CHAPTER 5

★ ★ ★

"OH MY GOD"

The car ride down I-95 from Baltimore to Washington in George Beall's sedan was uncomfortable on a number of counts. The temperature was climbing toward ninety on July 3, 1973, and the humidity was already 90 percent. Beall's Audi 100LS was a boxy affair, without much horsepower and without much air-conditioning oomph, and here were four grown men, one of whom stood six feet five, stuffed into its seats, understandably fidgety and uncomfortable. This was a day George Beall, Barney Skolnik, Tim Baker, and Ron Liebman had been anticipating with equal measures of excitement and anxiety; they were about to meet with the Big Boss of the entire U.S. Department of Justice, Attorney General Elliot Richardson.

The federal prosecutors stuffed into the Audi had been sitting on a big secret—one with national implications. And the decision on when exactly to tell the attorney general what they had discovered about Agnew had not been an easy one. "On the one hand, as soon as we have evidence against Agnew, it's perfectly clear to George and to us that this is something you need to report upstairs," says Tim Baker. "On the other hand, we didn't want to report it upstairs until we had our case pretty much in hand."

The Baltimore prosecutors' instincts had been to take the time to build the case to a point where it couldn't possibly be taken away from them, but they worried every day that something would leak to the press. A lot of people outside the U.S. Attorney's office in Baltimore had knowledge of the investigation. Skolnik, Baker, and Liebman had brought a lot of witnesses into the grand jury room, and every one of them had an attorney, or attorneys.

"If Richardson reads this in *The Washington Post* one morning and hasn't heard anything from Beall, we're all in a lot of trouble, and should be," says Baker.

Near the end of June, with the testimony from Lester Matz in the bag, Beall and his team determined that the case was finally ripe. It was time to tell all to Attorney General Richardson and to ask permission to pick the fruit.

Beall had been trying to get his team on the attorney general's calendar for almost two weeks and had actually managed to get on that busy calendar a few times. But always, at the last minute, somebody from Richardson's office had called to cancel. There were other, more pressing matters that took precedence. This was perfectly understandable, what with the two separate Watergate investigations now under way. But Beall and his team were growing impatient.

By July 3, the Baltimore prosecutors were unwilling to wait any longer. When Richardson's secretary had called in the morning to cancel a meeting scheduled for later that day, Beall refused to be put off. This was an emergency, he told the secretary, one he could not talk about over the phone. The attorney general needed to find some time in his schedule, that day, because the team from Baltimore was on its way. "George decides that no matter what they say, we're just going to go," Baker remembers.

Beall and his prosecutors spent the ride strategizing how to present their findings about the vice president to Richardson. They figured they had one shot, and not a lot of time, to make their case to the attorney general. Once they turned their findings over to Nixon's new handpicked man at Justice, the decision about how to proceed would be out of their control, and the prospects for moving forward would lean toward grim. At least that was how Barney Skolnik saw it.

Watergate investigators were already starting to turn up evidence that implicated Richard Nixon in a cover-up. So there was a perfectly reasonable case to be made that

the possibility of criminal charges against a sitting president *and* a sitting vice president would be too great a shock
for the country to absorb. "I had a very conscious realiza-
tion," Skolnik says, "not just that it was possible, but that
under all the circumstances it was highly likely that [At-
torney General Richardson] was going to say—perhaps for
the most honorable of reasons—'shut it down.'"

"I mean, he probably wouldn't say 'shut it down,' but he
could say words that would amount to 'shut it down.'"

ELLIOT RICHARDSON, at age fifty-two, was a veteran of the
Nixon administration. After an upright and distinguished
career in Massachusetts Republican politics—including a
stint as lieutenant governor—he had become Nixon's go-to
utility player for open cabinet posts in need of urgent fill-
ing. His first assignment was as secretary of the now-
defunct Department of Health, Education, and Welfare.
He next took over the Department of Defense, after Nixon
decided the previous secretary was insufficiently support-
ive of the escalation of the war in Vietnam. (Nixon had actually ordered the wiretapping of phones in his defense
secretary's office.)

In May 1973, the president asked Richardson to move
again, to what would be his third cabinet job in four years,
and easily the most pressure-packed position in the Nixon
administration at that moment. During an emotional
meeting at Camp David, Richardson later recalled, a visibly depressed Nixon "told me that I was more needed at
Justice than at Defense."

Nixon had gone through two attorney generals by then, both victims of the Watergate scandal. His first, John Mitchell, was eventually convicted and sent to prison for his role in the cover-up. His replacement, Richard Kleindienst, was forced from the job in Nixon's purge of the scapegoats at the end of April 1973—the same purge that saw the exit of the felons-to-be John Dean, H. R. Haldeman, and John Ehrlichman.

"He knew that Nixon was under a cloud," recalls one of Richardson's closest aides at the time, a young lawyer named J. T. Smith. "He knew that the mood in the White House on the part of the president and his staff was quite bleak."

Richardson took the job, in spite of the outlook. There was no shortage of hot seats in Washington during the second term of the Nixon administration, but none was hotter than the attorney general's. Watergate was already a three-alarm fire when Richardson took office in May 1973, and by early July the blaze had grown considerably worse.

President Nixon's recently canned White House counsel, John Dean, had begun his dramatic testimony in front of the Senate Watergate Committee on June 25, 1973. Dean's six-hour, 245-page opening statement was akin to a crime novel, and the author fingered Nixon as one of the culprits. The president knew of the burglary, Dean explained, and a slew of other dirty tricks against his political opponents, and had been complicit in obstructing the investigations into the crimes. Dean had begged absolution for his old boss. "It is my honest belief, that while the president was involved, that he did not realize or appreciate at any time the implications of his involvement. And I think that when the facts come out, I hope the president is forgiven." But Congress did not seem to be in a forgiving mood; it had direct evidence that the president had abused the power of his office for personal ends. And Congress wasn't alone.

Archibald Cox, the special prosecutor Richardson had just appointed, was beginning to work up a serious case against the president, too. And he was very interested in Dean's assistance for his own investigation. Worried about death threats against the former Nixon aide, Special Prosecutor Cox had asked the U.S. marshals to keep Dean and his wife under armed, round-the-clock protection.

That was the lay of the land at noon, on July 3, 1973, when Richardson learned there were four officials from the U.S. Attorney's Office for the District of Maryland waiting anxiously in his anteroom, and apparently there with news about an entirely new "emergency."

"So we get there, we're ushered up to the attorney general's office, which to say 'impressive' is to understate it," remembers Ron Liebman. "And we wait and we wait."

Until, finally . . .

"Richardson comes in and he's annoyed," Tim Baker says. "You know, 'What's so important that you're interrupting my day and you won't even tell my secretary what it's about? What's so important?'"

Beall started talking fast, executing the strategy the four men had finalized on the ride down. He began his presentation by introducing his team, one by one, detailing their résumés so Richardson wouldn't get hung up on the team's obvious youth.

"George talks about himself," Liebman recalls, "University of Virginia Law School, he knew his brother was a senator. He turns to [Barney] says, 'This is Barney Skolnik.' And Elliot Richardson is making notes: 'Barney Skolnik went to Harvard College, Harvard Law School, was in the Justice Department, senior prosecutor, very experienced.' 'This is Tim Baker.' He looks at Tim Baker, starts making notes: 'Tim Baker went to Williams College. He went to Harvard Law School. He was on the *Harvard Law Review*. He clerked for the chief judge of the Fourth Circuit Court of Appeals. He clerked for the chief justice of the United States.' Richardson is making notes. [George] says, 'This is Ron Liebman.' And George said, 'He went to Western Maryland College,' and before he even got to University of Maryland Law School, Richardson puts his pen down and looks at me. Stops taking notes. And to my dying day, I will remember thinking, 'He's looking at me; he's thinking one of two things: either 'what the hell are *you* doing here?' or 'good for you!' And I didn't know which, but he stopped taking notes!"

"He's sitting there," Tim Baker says, "but then more doodling and more and more impatient! And just at the point where we're sure [George is going to get to Agnew], the secretary comes in and gives him a note! He just up and leaves, no explanation, just gets up and leaves."

"The minute he leaves," Liebman says, "of course we're saying, 'George, say this, say that!'"

Richardson returned several minutes later, and Beall launched into a circuitous explanation of the Baltimore County investigation. "When George gets a little closer to the vice president," says Liebman, "another note comes in. Elliot Richardson gets up and he leaves. Doesn't say 'excuse me.'"

Richardson eventually acknowledged that he was summoned to the phone in the first instance by Alexander Haig, Nixon's new White House chief of staff, and in the second instance by Nixon himself. Nixon was furious. The president had seen news reports that Richardson's handpicked special prosecutor, Archibald Cox, was nosing around Nixon's private real estate deals. Nixon wanted Richardson to order Cox to put out a press release denying that he was looking into the financing of Nixon's purchases of his properties in Key Biscayne, Florida, and San Clemente, California. Pronto!

"That's all going on outside of our hearing," Liebman says. "And the attorney general of the United States has got these guys in there—three of whom are kids—from Baltimore. And he came back in, and *finally* George got to the meat of the matter."

"We have evidence that Vice President Agnew took bribes as county executive, governor, and even as vice president," Baker recalls Beall saying.

Richardson perked up at that. *Even as vice president.* Finally, they had the attorney general's full attention.

"It was my job to lay out the evidence we had," remembers Baker. "And [the attorney general] is very interested in the evidence. What he, of course, wants to know is, how good a case is this? And it's a good case. I mean, we've got good stuff and we know it. I just start banging away on 'so-and-so will testify, and he's got documents, and he's backed up by . . . ' Nail after nail after nail after nail."

While Baker talked, the rest of the team was trying to get a read on Richardson. "If you're asking me if I got the impression that he was surprised, the answer is no," says Barney Skolnik. "If you were sentient in those days, you had a sense of what kind of a human being the vice president was. And Elliot Richardson, to put it mildly, was sentient." Unsurprised, perhaps, but clearly far from sanguine about what he was hearing.

"I read [Richardson's] expression as saying, 'I need this right now like I need another hole in the head,'" says Liebman.

At that moment, a little after noon, July 3, 1973, Elliot Richardson had been in the job of attorney general for a grand total of thirty-nine days and was already overseeing the most sensitive criminal probe, maybe, in the history of the Justice Department. And here were these barely out-of-law-school prosecutors, none of whom he had ever laid eyes on before, saying, "We know you're investigating the president, but we need you to investigate the vice president as well." They needed his blessing for a freaking criminal investigation against Spiro T. Agnew, the most combative man in the White House. (And that was saying something in 1973.) Anybody watching the vice president in action the last five years knew he was sure to fight back like a cornered marmot.

If you were the attorney general, how many pitched

battles would you be willing to fight at the same time? What would you do?

Here's what Elliot Richardson did: He told the prosecutors that "he was greatly concerned for the nation if these allegations proved to be accurate, particularly in view of the Watergate matter," Tim Baker wrote in a memo to file after the meeting. "However, he unequivocally stated that the allegations must be fully investigated."

"What he did," says Liebman, "was, he started crawling into the case. 'What about this? What are you going to do about that?' Like he was a collaborator with us, which he was. It was extraordinary."

Attorney General Elliot Richardson

Elliot Richardson's momentous decision, made without hesitation, has stuck with the prosecutors, even decades later. "We don't know him," Skolnik remembers. "I mean, I've heard good things about him, but we don't know him, and it's very much with a great sense of anxiety that we are going to say to him, 'Here, what do you want us to do?' and then, figuratively speaking, hold our breath until he tells us what he's going to tell us."

Fighting back tears, Skolnik continues, "I knew—I think we all knew—that we were in the presence of a very special human being."

Richardson was taking on the responsibility of overseeing active criminal investigations into the president and the vice president . . . at the same time. This was two entirely *separate* cases. This was Nobody Is Above the Law, squared. The Baltimore office would continue to work the case, Richardson said. Beall and his team needed to keep going, keep digging, keep building the case against Agnew. But he wanted it done in absolute secrecy. Nobody outside this room, Richardson implored, could know. The clear mission, while never explicitly voiced, was to pry the vice president of the United States from office before it was too late. Before he could ascend to the presidency.

"We were all about now: You've got this completely corrupt guy as vice president of the United States," says Baker. "We've got to do this right; we can't make any mistakes here."

Richardson's own top aide, J. T. Smith, has very clear memories of that day also. Most vivid of all is Richardson coming out of the meeting when it was finally over, shellshocked, muttering something nobody was meant to hear: "Oh my God."

CHAPTER 6

★ ★ ★

THE PRUDENT COURSE

Richard Nixon was obsessed with his own physical health, unusually proud of his ability to ward off illnesses large and small. And as president, let the record show, he really had proven healthy as a horse. Early in 1973, right around the time of his sixtieth birthday, Nixon had reportedly asked his aides to find out if any other president in the history of the Republic had gone through an entire term without taking a sick day—as he had. He had earned the right to brag. And he did. "I've been blessed with a strong physical makeup," the president said. "I never had a headache in my life." Give the man a gold star.

That extraordinary run of presidential good health was interrupted on July 12, 1973. The president woke that morning with a "stabbing" pain in the right side of his chest. Summoned to the presidential bedroom that morning, Chief of Staff Alexander Haig grew alarmed by what he saw. "[Nixon's] skin was pasty, his eyes bloodshot and feverish, his voice weak, his breathing shallow," Haig wrote. "He coughed spasmodically and the pain this caused him showed in his face. He sat up in bed, clutching his chest, and I noticed that his pillowcase was spotted with blood."

Loath to mar his perfect attendance record, Nixon tried to tough it out. He hauled himself out of his sickbed and put in a full day's work. But by nightfall, the White House medical staff was nervous; they rushed Nixon to the hospital, where doctors found his fever had spiked to 102 degrees. The diagnosis was pneumonia. The prognosis was, well, wait and see. Haig was even more shaken than he had been that morning. He'd served in the military for more than twenty years, and had seen a thing or two in that time, in both Korea and Vietnam; he said the president's condition looked "life-threatening." This assessment remained entirely private.

Nixon ended up hospitalized for a full week, and the evening newscasts filled with updates on his condition: he was suffering "pain in his right lung"; he wasn't sleeping much; his temperature was still too high. Nixon's doctor addressed the media from the hospital, telling the American people in somber tones that the president was "a sick man."

It's never a good thing to have a president hospitalized, much less for an entire week. And this was no ordinary time. This was July 1973. The Summer of Watergate.

The day after Nixon was rushed to the hospital, a White House aide named Alexander Butterfield informed the Senate committee investigating Watergate of a recording system in the White House, revealing the existence of thousands of hours of tapes of the president's conversations. The tapes could be incriminating. The White House staff was concerned. The Senate committee was concerned. The special prosecutor was concerned.

But one man was more concerned than anyone else in the nation's capital, and that man was Attorney General Elliot Richardson.

What if this illness was something worse than garden-variety pneumonia? What if Nixon's illness really was life threatening? What if the president was cracking under the strain of Watergate? There were what-ifs enough to keep Richardson up all night. Because just ten days earlier he had been told that the next man up, Vice President Spiro Agnew, appeared to be running an active criminal operation, taking thousands of dollars of cash bribes, from inside the White House. *Oh my God.*

"Richardson was quite worried about the overall mental and physical health of Nixon," says his former aide J. T. Smith. "There were rumors that (a) he was drinking heavily, and (b) he was out of his mind. . . . [Richardson] knew it wasn't a good scene, to the point where he didn't think it tolerable to have Agnew remain in the line of succession."

Richardson and his own team at the Justice Department already knew the stakes. George Beall and his team knew. A few key witnesses like Lester Matz knew. But no one else in the country knew just what kind of man was Spiro Agnew. And the fact of a very unhealthy President Nixon lying flat on his back in the National Naval Medical Center in Bethesda, Maryland, added urgency to the mission of ousting Spiro Agnew from office. Speed mattered more than ever now.

"It really was 'We're all in this together and we gotta figure out what to do for the country because this is some heavy shit,'" Barney Skolnik recalls. "We're talking about the summer of '73; Watergate hearings are going on. Everybody was conscious that Nixon, aside from being a 'crook,' in his memorable word, might not last."

★ ★ ★

IN THE MIDST of those very heavy prospects, some good news ended up rolling in the door at the U.S. Attorney's office in Baltimore. The prosecutors had brought on board another key cooperator, Jerome B. "Jerry" Wolff. By the middle of July, Wolff was helping to lock down the case against Agnew. He was an engineer by trade and had paid a few kickbacks to Agnew when he was county executive in Baltimore County. When Agnew became governor, he recruited Wolff to be the chairman-director of the State Roads Commission. The appointment had upset one of their mutual friends, a big-time real estate developer and mortgage broker named I. H. "Bud" Hammerman. Wolff had been doing the engineering on Bud Hammerman's private projects in Maryland, and Hammerman didn't want to lose him to some state government sinecure. But Agnew essentially told Hammerman to quit his whining. "You won't lose by it," he told the developer. And then he made sure of it. Agnew concocted a scheme by which he, Wolff, and Hammerman would all profit from Wolff's new state job, at least in the short run. At least until they got caught.

It was Hammerman who came knocking on Jerry Wolff's door to outline the key elements of Agnew's plan. It wasn't exactly rocket science; it was based on a long-standing game that was already in play at the statehouse. Engineering firms had been paying kickbacks for state contracts for years, and they knew exactly who had to be paid. The authority to grant each and every contract for road and bridge construction was vested in the State Roads Commission, subject only to approval by the governor. The governor controlled the whole thing. This was like Baltimore County, only bigger. So Agnew wanted to scale up his operation, and to scale up his efforts at conceal-ment. "It was explained to him you want a 'bag man,'" Liebman says. "You don't want to take directly; you want to insulate yourself." It was the prudent course. If accusa-tions were made, Agnew would have some distance be-tween himself and the contractor paying the bribe. He could plead ignorance or, at the very least, retain plausible deniability. Hammerman was to be Agnew's bag man.

When Hammerman laid out Agnew's plan to Wolff, the new head of the State Roads Commission was all in. Wolff would oversee the bidding process, award the contracts, run it by Agnew, and then alert Hammerman as to the winners. Then Hammerman would collect the kickback.

"Over the course of 18 to 20 months, the scheme was fully implemented," Skolnik, Baker, and Liebman would report. Wolff kept Hammerman informed as to which engineers were to receive state contracts, and Hammerman kept Wolff informed as to which engineers were making cash payments. It was soon generally understood among engineers that Hammerman was the person to see in connection with state roads engineering contracts. Engineering firms would inform Hammerman of their interest in obtaining state work, and Hammerman would reply that he would see what he could do. In some cases, an engineer would specify the particular work in which he was interested; in most cases, the engineers would not specify any particular job.

"There was no need for Hammerman to make coarse demands or to issue threats because the engineers clearly indicated that they knew what was expected of them. The discussions were generally about 'political contributions,' but the conversations left no doubt that the engineers understood exactly how the system worked—that is, that cash payments to the Governor through Hammerman were necessary in order for their companies to receive substantial state contracts."

When Wolff and Hammerman were still engineering

their three-man extortion ring, Wolff suggested that they split the proceeds evenly among themselves. Agnew was not enthusiastic about the proposed arrangement. He didn't see why Wolff should get any of the money, he told Hammerman. Governor Agnew settled on this: He would take 50 percent. Hammerman and Wolff could split the rest between themselves. So Agnew pocketed 50 percent of the bribe money; Jerry Wolff got 25 percent; Bud Hammerman kept the remaining 25 percent.

"The deal was the contractor would pay Hammerman," Liebman says. "He's holding the money and paying the money directly to Agnew."

Hammerman opened up a safe-deposit box at a local bank and would deliver the money to Agnew as needed. The two men worked out a coded language, just in case their phones were tapped. Each thousand dollars they took in was a "paper." When Governor Agnew was in need of cash, he'd call Hammerman and ask how many "papers" he had, and his bag man would then deliver however much he wanted.

Agnew, in addition to going through Bud Hammerman, occasionally took money directly. From old discreet pals like Lester Matz and Allen Green. Why give up a percentage to the bag man, even if Bud was a friend? "He was greedy," Liebman says of Agnew, "absolutely greedy."

And, speaking of greed, Wolff used some of the bribery money he accepted to pay off other public officials to obtain work for a pair of consulting firms in which he had his own financial interest. Call it re-bribing.

Jerry Wolff was, by his own admission, one venal SOB.

But he was also fastidious in his bookkeeping. "Wolff kept detailed contemporaneous documents on which he recorded dates, amounts, engineering firms, sources of the moneys that he received from Hammerman as his share of the proceeds," the prosecutors noted. Wolff had turned all of these notebooks over to the U.S. Attorney's office in Baltimore, and the nervous prosecutors, just to be certain, sent them to lab specialists at the Bureau of Alcohol, Tobacco, and Firearms to have the ink on each page dated and tested for authenticity. When the results came back, Wolff's gold mine of documentary evidence was deemed real.

DATE	AMOUNT	REMARKS
5/1/67 - 12/31/67	450	in Baltimore
5/1/67 - 12/31/67	750	in Nassau (1 - 15)
5/1/67 - 12/31/67	150	in Ocean Reef (3 - 1)
5/1/67 - 12/31/67	1500	
5/1/67 - 12/31/67	3000	S. Slavin #1
5/1/67 - 12/31/67	300	
6/21/68	1500	S. Slavin #2
10/2/68	1500	Smith Avenue
10/30/68	9000	Goucher Blvd.
6/10/69	7500	Pmt #3 Rt. 28 prop
7/10/69	6000	Gudelsby

Lester Matz's payments to Jerry Wolff, as reflected in Wolff's documents

Even with testimony from Matz and Wolff and ultimately even Hammerman in the bag, Richardson was not entirely satisfied with the case against Vice President Agnew. The attorney general also favored the prudent course. Richardson and the prosecutors had already decided to focus their efforts on the witnesses who were actually implicated in the scheme and likely to be convicted if they went to trial. But Richardson wanted something more from those witnesses than sworn testimony and contemporaneous diaries. He directed that each of the prosecutors' key witnesses submit to a polygraph exam by FBI agents, to ensure that their testimonies could be trusted. The Baltimore team was confident their informants had been truthful, but the lie detector gambit was anxiety inducing—for witnesses and prosecutors alike.

"We had been assigned this FBI lie detector specialist," says Ron Liebman, "who—when he met with the prosecutors—said to us, 'I'm gonna prove these guys are lying.' And we were saying, 'No, no, no, no! We don't want you to do that! We want you to tell us *whether* they're lying, but don't *prove* that they're lying!' And the guy said, 'Absolutely, I understand. One hundred percent. When I'm finished with them, I'm gonna show you where they're lying.'"

The prosecutors had deliberately kept the FBI out of the investigation, having opted to use the IRS instead. Now the G-men were threatening to upend all of their careful work. "Holy cow, this is it," Liebman remembers thinking, all these months into the investigation. "This is where we're gonna screw up this entire case."

Liebman and his colleagues were not in the room as the agent administering the test instructed Wolff to take off his suit jacket and roll up his sleeve, and attached the already nervous engineer to the polygraph machine. They were not in the room when the agent began the questioning.

"Have you intentionally given the Government any false information about the corruption investigation?

"Are you now withholding any information whatsoever about your part in this kickback setup?"

After a pause in the test, the FBI agent wrote in his notes that Jerry Wolff appeared "visibly upset. He said he knew he had not done well. He said he could 'feel' the reactions occur" as he gave his answers. He was in "such an emotional state," the lie detector specialist recorded, "that it was no longer possible to continue."

The prosecutors, waiting nearby, were alerted that something had gone wrong. "The FBI guy came into our room," Liebman recalls, "and he said, 'You better get in here. This guy, he's having a nervous breakdown! He's really having a nervous breakdown.'"

The polygraph test had only just begun, and it appeared that the train might already be coming off the tracks.

Liebman, George Beall, and Wolff's attorney spoke with Wolff in private, and soon learned exactly what had sent the polygraph readings spiking in every direction. "It turns out," Liebman says, "what Jerry Wolff was lying about . . . was an affair. Nothing to do with the case at all. I remember Jerry Wolff laughing nervously and hysterically crying at the same time, with his one sleeve rolled up, still attached to this machine, and I felt so bad for him."

Wolff and all of the other witnesses did eventually pass their polygraph tests, save for a few tense moments. And once the results were in, the attorney general decided it

was time to take the next big step, a step that would certainly change everything.

On August 1, 1973, George Beall hand delivered a letter
to Judah Best, a high-end defense attorney who had been
retained several months earlier by Vice President Spiro
Agnew, no doubt out of an abundance of caution. Beall
was well aware that the vice president had laid on legal
representation, because Jud Best had started badgering
Beall aggressively, pressing for any hint about where the
Baltimore County investigation was heading. Best had
even called Beall at home one Saturday morning, demanding information, because, he said, "my guy is hopping up
and down." Beall had given the defense lawyer non-
answers that day, as he had every other day, right until August 1, when he personally handed Best a letter that
dispensed with the careful non-answers and got right to
the devastating point.

"This office is now conducting an investigation of allegations concerning possible violations by your client and
others of federal criminal statutes," the letter began. The
vice president's alleged crimes, Beall wrote, were of the
highest severity, and included potential "extortion," "bribery," "conspiracy," and violations of tax law.

This was not just a courtesy heads-up to Agnew's lawyer. It was a direct request from the U.S. Attorney's office
to the vice president of the United States for a cache of
documents related to Agnew's possible criminal activities.
The nature and scope of the request was not just compre-
hensive but bordering on proctologic: "All bank statements, cancelled checks, check vouchers, check stubs,

check books, deposit tickets, and savings account books . . . for any and all checking and savings bank accounts in the United States and elsewhere." If Agnew wished to cooperate, Beall explained, he had a little over a week to have the documents delivered to Baltimore.

If, on the other hand, "he believes that the materials might tend to incriminate him," Agnew was free to assert his Fifth Amendment rights.

The note was brief and to the point, but its historical weight was hard to miss. The sitting vice president, his lawyer was hereby informed, was at very real risk of criminal indictment. "I remember when we handed that letter to Jud Best," says Ron Liebman. "He took it. And he said, 'I feel like jumping out the window.'"

★ ★ ★

IN THE FIRST week of August 1973, the defense attorney Martin London had just wrapped a high-profile case representing Jackie Kennedy, the former First Lady, in a battle with a paparazzi photographer who had harassed her and her children to the point of Secret Service intervention. London was a partner at the time in the white-shoe New York City law firm Paul, Weiss. Another partner in the firm, Jay Topkis, a sought-after specialist in criminal tax cases, came to Marty London that week with a pitch for a high-profile new client for the both of them. The way Jay put it, it was a pitch that Marty would never forget.

"He says to me, 'Marty, I just got the strangest call,'" London remembers. "'A fella calls me and he says he's from Chuck Colson's firm in Washington, D.C. And he asks me if I can come to Washington, D.C., tomorrow morning to meet a new client.'"

Chuck Colson was a former White House lawyer who would himself later be sent to prison for his role in the 1972 campaign's "dirty tricks." But that August—a year before he got his prison stripes—Colson was a lawyer in private practice, and his firm had a client who needed additional high-powered representation fast. The kind you might find at Paul, Weiss.

As Topkis explained the call, Marty London assumed they were about to get sucked into defending some new figure or other who was about to emerge from the Watergate investigations. But Topkis was slow to get to the bottom line, choosing instead to recite a blow-by-blow of the call. Who was the client? Topkis had asked the caller. "I can't mention his name on the phone, it's so confidential, I'm not allowed to mention his name," he said.

"Okay," Topkis said. "Well, *what* is he?"

"A very high government official," the caller said.

"Is he a congressman?"

"Higher."

"Is he a senator?"

"Higher."

"Oh my goodness, is he a cabinet official?"

"Higher."

"Oh my God, you're talking about the president of the United States!" Topkis finally exclaimed.

The caller replied, "Well—not quite so high."

The potential new client, Topkis told London, finally, was Spiro Agnew.

"Is there any reason we shouldn't represent this guy?" Topkis asked.

London was taking it all in. His bottom line was—the bottom line.

"Are we gonna get paid?" London asked.

"Yes," said Topkis.

"Then there's no reason we shouldn't represent him," London said.

A few days later, London and Topkis traveled from New York to Washington to sit down for the first time with their new (paying) client. The meeting came at what was, undoubtedly, the most perilous moment in Spiro Agnew's political life and career. He had just been formally notified five days earlier—in the letter from U.S. Attorney George Beall—that he was under investigation for bribery and extortion. Conviction carried with it the possibility of serious time in prison, maybe years. And a handful of his co-conspirators, it seemed, were already spilling what they knew. Jud Best was a fine attorney, but this required a lot of additional brainpower.

"We were with the vice president for about an hour," London says. "And at some point, he called the president. Or the president called him, I don't remember. I could hear the timbre of Richard Nixon's voice. It was not on speakerphone, so I could hear him speaking to the vice president, [but] had no idea what he said."

A few minutes after Nixon got off the phone, Attorney

General Elliot Richardson came knocking at Agnew's door, asking if he might join the discussion.

Richardson, in fact, had walked straight over from a meeting in President Nixon's office, where he had just spent an uncomfortable few minutes briefing the president on the vice president's situation. According to handwritten notes from the Oval Office meeting, Richardson had told Nixon, who was still recovering from his recent bout with pneumonia, that "indictments are certain unless there is a miraculous answer [by Agnew] to the anticipated testimony" of witnesses.

These witnesses, the attorney general had told Nixon, "have little or no motive to implicate [Agnew]," and the testimony they had given the Justice Department was already "damning." The U.S. Attorney in Maryland was thoroughly "convinced" by the evidence and was not, in Richardson's words, "the captive of zealots on his staff." Nixon was probably relieved that he had ordered the White House taping system disconnected three weeks earlier.

After that sobering briefing, Nixon asked Richardson to walk over and meet with Agnew and his lawyers immediately. They deserved to know where the investigation stood.

Richardson did not play coy with the vice president and his legal team. "He said, 'Look, this is a serious case,'" London recalls. "'It's not a political putsch. There is serious evidence.'"

Richardson's own contemporaneous account of the meeting matches London's, and goes a bit further. "I told the Vice President that I was there at the request of the

President," he wrote in a memo to file, "in order to give him a summary of the status of an investigation being conducted by the U.S. Attorney for the District of Maryland." When he informed Agnew that the prosecution had witnesses who "could testify to having made payments directly to the Vice President," Agnew grew irate.

"The Vice President remarked at various points that the whole thing was a fabrication, that [Lester] Matz was crazy," Richardson wrote, and "he particularly stressed his lack of confidence in the objectivity of the U.S. Attorney and his staff, implying that if the investigation were being conducted by a more 'objective' team, his reaction might be different."

Richardson figured that last point, about the prosecutors, was where Agnew was sure to train his fire. Those early surprise subpoenas and the interrupt-a-man's-martini tactics by which they were served would be a toehold for Agnew in his first efforts to vilify the prosecutors and the case against him. "In the light of the various instances of arrogance that had come to his attention . . . he believed that U.S. Attorney Beall had lost control of the investigation," Richardson wrote. "He therefore asked that the prosecution be placed in the hands of an experienced professional prosecutor."

Richardson explained to Agnew that Beall's "demeanor, sincerity, and professionalism had been very impressive to me," but the attorney general also knew enough to be wary of the vice president. Agnew was already signaling that he was willing to employ a scorched-earth survival strategy. The allegations against him were "fabrications," the witnesses against him were "crazy," and the prosecutors were "zealous" and out to get him. It was a witch hunt.

★ ★ ★

AT FIVE O'CLOCK that afternoon, having returned to the Department of Justice, Richardson put out a call for backup. He summoned to his office Henry E. Petersen, the assistant attorney general in charge of the Criminal Division. Petersen, tanned and rested on his first day back after a peaceful vacation on his boat, knew not a single whit about the Agnew investigation. He was already up to his ears in Watergate. He was scheduled to testify before the Senate committee the next day. But now, Richardson said, he needed Petersen to undertake a full review of the case down in Baltimore. He wanted him to re-interview every single witness against Agnew; he further wanted Petersen's professional assessment of the office in Baltimore and of their work product. The attorney general then ushered Petersen out of the office with a combination apology and warning: "You're going to be sorry you came back from vacation."

CHAPTER 7

"I HAVE NO INTENTION TO BE SKEWERED IN THIS FASHION"

B arney Skolnik happened to be the person who answered the phone when the *Wall Street Journal* reporter Jerry Landauer called the U.S. Attorney's office in
Baltimore. Landauer already had his scoop; he just needed
a comment. You know, on the Agnew investigation. "I remember coming into Barney's office," Liebman recalls,

"and he's on the phone with Landauer and he mouthed to me, 'They've got it.'"

Landauer was an old hand with a long track record of enterprise reporting on corruption in government and business. For a couple of years at least, he had been noodling around the rumors of Spiro Agnew's kickback scheme during his time in office in Maryland, but he had never had enough to run with a story, until now. Among other things, Landauer seemed to have the letter George Beall had sent to Agnew's personal attorney a few days earlier. He said he was still waiting for a statement from the vice president's office before going with the story, but he wasn't going to wait much longer. And he didn't.

"Vice President Spiro T. Agnew was formally notified by the Justice Department last week that he is a target of a far-ranging criminal investigation by the U.S. attorney's office in Baltimore," was his lede in the first edition of *The Wall Street Journal* on August 7, 1973. "The allegations against him include bribery, extortion and tax fraud." *The Washington Post* was right behind, with a story co-authored by Carl Bernstein. Both news stories included a statement from Agnew: "I will make no further comment until the investigation has been completed, other than to say that I am innocent of any wrongdoing, that I have confidence in the criminal justice system of the United States, and that I am equally confident my innocence will be affirmed."

The story caught the rest of the national press corps off guard, and they scrambled to catch up. "Washington was stunned today by the disclosure that Vice President Agnew is under criminal investigation," NBC's John Chancellor led that night. "Involved are possible charges of bribery, extortion, and tax evasion. . . . Agnew says he is innocent, a member of his staff said today you are probably going to hear more that is terribly serious."

The investigation's existence was news even to many on Agnew's White House staff. David Keene, a top political aide, who was supposed to be enjoying a vacation in South Carolina, took a panicked call from a fellow staffer. Keene had to get on a plane and come back to Washington. Now! The vice president was thinking about canceling his entire schedule. "What?!" said Keene. The aide filled him in, and Keene packed his bags.

The sudden disclosure of the investigation was even more disruptive to the Baltimore prosecutors. And even more galling. They could no longer conduct their work in the shadows: they were in the national spotlight, for better or worse. Mostly for worse.

"It took about three seconds for the American press to attack the federal courthouse," says Liebman. "The FBI came in and talked to us about how we had to secure our files and put them in lead file cabinets, and I had to take my name out of the directory assistance—the phone books in those days. None of which we did. We told them, 'Yeah, okay. You know, we really don't have the time for that right now!'"

Their nondescript offices inside the courthouse, wholly devoid of any semblance of modern security, became a magnet for intrepid reporters hoping to overhear some newsworthy nugget about the case. Barney Skolnik appealed to George Beall to maintain order. "I strongly suggest that, if at all possible," Skolnik wrote, "some place other than right *next* to our office receptionist be set up for the press to lounge during the day." He had seen people relevant to the investigation whispering to the receptionist "while ten or fifteen members of the press listen to the conversation." As an additional measure, the ever-vigilant Skolnik suggested, the prosecutors should have all of their phones—in the office and at home—"checked for bugs as soon as possible."

Ron Liebman, his home number still listed in the Baltimore phone book, realized how relentless the press was when he received a late-night call from a reporter desperate to speak to Beall. He "woke me up: 'You've got to give me his home number! You got to give me a phone number!'" When Liebman refused, the reporter pressed, "'Listen, this is really important, Ron, you have to understand this. If you don't give me his home number, I'm going to go to his house and I'm going to wake him up.' And I said, 'Great, have a nice trip!'"

Hopes the pressure would die down a bit were exploded almost immediately, by Spiro Agnew himself. The day after the story broke, Agnew made clear that he would fight his case in the court of public opinion. And of course, because he was Agnew, he knew that the best defense would be a good offense. So the vice president called a press conference and went on the attack—against the prosecutors. "Because of defamatory statements that are being leaked to the news media by sources that the news reports refer to as close to the Federal investigation, I cannot adhere to my original intention to remain silent following my initial statement," he announced at the top. "I have no intention to be skewered in this fashion. And since I have no intention to be so skewered, I have called this press conference to label as false and scurrilous and malicious these rumors, these assertions and accusations that are being circulated." He called the allegations against him "damned lies"; denied receiving a single solitary kickback from "any person, contractor or company doing business with the State of Maryland or with the Federal Government"; asserted that he had not and would not obstruct the investigation; said that he had informed President Nixon, who had offered his support "unequivocally."

Most of all, and more than once, Agnew expressed his deep disappointment in the leaks and implied that those leaks were coming from the U.S. Attorney's office in Baltimore. Clearly, those prosecutors had an ax to grind.

Agnew received a note from a supporter who had watched his remarks from nearby in the West Wing. "That was one hell of a press conference," Pat Buchanan wrote. He added, "Noli Illegitimis Carborundum," a Latin phrase that translates to "Don't let the bastards grind you down."

Agnew fired off a response, assuring his friend, "I'll watch out for the illegitimis."

Agnew's play seemed to work, judging from the mail. Bribery, extortion, cash payoffs in the White House—these accusations were all now public. But Republicans across the country really didn't seem to mind! In fact, they seemed to regard it as a badge of honor, won by Sir Spiro for his willingness to joust with those radic-libs.

The vice president's office received hundreds of letters

from supporters all across the country. There are boxes and boxes of these missives held in Agnew's files at the University of Maryland, those he received and the replies sent. "Dear Mr. Vice President—We believe in your innocence," a couple from Kansas City wrote. "Give them hell—the press and the liberals are out to get you and all conservatives."

"I'm sick of what the media and the Democrats are doing," a schoolteacher from Colorado offered. "They lost and [they] can't take it."

Joe Taylor from Missouri wrote, "Dear Veep, Give the God damned sons-of-bitches hell. It's a good thing somebody in Washington has guts enough to say something, and fight back."

Agnew wrote back to that one: "Dear Mr. Taylor: Thank you for your very kind letter—and for your excellent advice! Warm regards."

Among David Keene's jobs on his hurried return from vacation was to shore up Agnew's political standing on Capitol Hill, a task that proved not very difficult. Republicans in Congress rushed to Agnew's defense, despite what you might think would be political peril in providing cover for an executive officer accused of serious crimes. "[They] were hearing from their constituents that 'this is our guy!'" says Keene.

"The man has been put under incredible pressure," the Conservative Party senator James Buckley of New York protested to reporters. Agnew was being convicted via "trial by print," slandered by "thirdhand leaks of information that may or may not be sound."

It was all an "injustice," said Senator Bob Dole of Kansas. Of the allegations themselves, Dole said, "We really don't know what the facts may be."

On the steps of the Capitol, Carl Curtis of Nebraska went one step further. "To condemn someone, to have innuendos, to raise questions—'When is he going to retire? Will he be impeached?'—when no one has made a specific charge against him, damages him all across the country. And, furthermore, it's damaging our country." Even the *discussion* that Agnew might be in trouble—in the words of this Republican senator—was "damaging" to the country. Curtis was downright conspiratorial in cast, suggesting that there was an illicit "scheme on" from some "sadistic element" to destroy Nixon and take down his number two in the process.

Agnew wasn't the only person in the capital accumulating mail from vice presidential supporters. Attorney General Elliot Richardson's office also began to fill up with mail. "I hope you and all your smart Justice Department lawyers are pleased," one woman wrote that fall. "You have done a great wrong to this nation and one day you are going to have to pay."

"Are you a Democrat, or has this been done by the Democrat Party?" a woman from Lubbock, Texas, asked. "If so, that explains it, for it looks like they can't bear for the Republicans to get any glory or praise for anything."

"I believe there is deliberate malice," another man wrote, "from the liberal news media and also from politicians who fear Mr. Agnew's appeal to the average American."

The Agnew stew simmered on at a low boil for the next

few weeks, while the vice president himself remained fairly quiet. He retreated to Palm Springs for a golf weekend with his friend Frank Sinatra, who had made his personal attorney available to Agnew to provide legal advice.

The relative calm ended when a new edition of *Time* magazine hit the newsstands: "Despite all the Vice President's protestations of innocence, however, *Time* has learned that in the view of Justice Department officials in Washington, the case against him is growing steadily stronger, and that an indictment appears inevitable." Agnew blew. He called another press conference and renewed his attack. The past few weeks had convinced him the leakers were unquestionably "persons involved in the investigatory process" who have "decided to indict me in the press whether or not the evidence supports their position. This is a clear and outrageous effort to influence the outcome of possible grand jury deliberations. . . . I will fight. I will fight to prove my innocence and I intend to remain in the high office to which I have been twice elected." Agnew took no follow-up questions after he had read his statement. But he did release to the press a letter he had sent to Attorney General Elliot Richardson: "Some personnel of your Department have regularly released information to the press—when their duty was to maintain silence.

"There can be no doubt that you now have the obligation to investigate these leaks and to use all the tools at your disposal to expose and discipline those responsible. Only drastic and immediate action will curb this vicious and illegal practice."

The vice president was turning the tables—or trying to,

at least. Forget Agnew's crimes and the ever-growing mountain of admissible evidence proving them; to hear him tell it, it was these dirty prosecutors who were corrupting the justice system. It was time to investigate the investigators.

And President Nixon agreed! He did not appreciate his vice president being buried under unsourced "innuendo" and leaks. "I will say this," Nixon told reporters at his nationally televised press conference the next day. "Any individual in the Justice Department or in the prosecutor's office who is in the employ of the United States, who has leaked information in this case, to the press or to anybody else, will be summarily dismissed from Government service. That's how strongly I feel about this."

Elliot Richardson announced that he would conduct a "full-scale" internal investigation to find any leakers at Justice. "I have today asked the Acting Assistant Attorney General for Administration, who has had no prior involvement in this investigation, to undertake a systematic inquiry using any and all departmental resources he sees fit," Richardson wrote, in responding to Agnew's official letter of complaint. "I have also asked the director of the F.B.I. to cooperate by making available F.B.I. personnel to assist in the inquiry as needed."

You think the FBI might upset some applecarts looking into bribery in some out-in-the-provinces county government? Just wait and see what they could do when wielded against the Justice Department itself, and at the direct and personal insistence of both the president and the vice president of the United States.

CHAPTER 8

★ ★ ★

"IS HE A GOOD BOY?"

Barney Skolnik, Tim Baker, and Ron Liebman were handed questionnaires to complete, under penalty of perjury. "Have you made comments to anyone about: the substance or weight of the potential evidence against the Vice President? The veracity of potential witnesses whose testimony might be prejudicial to the Vice President?" As if they had time for this.

"It really was ludicrous," Barney Skolnik says. "I mean,

we're investigating the case and suddenly people are coming from Washington . . . and saying, 'Here, this is an affidavit about whether or not you have leaked and you must fill it out and you must sign it.' Everybody! I mean, it wasn't just—it was the secretaries. It was [everyone]."

In the end, no Justice Department officials were found to have leaked. This outrage about leaks to the press was fine and good as a public relations strategy for Agnew and the White House, and maybe it could carry some water as a legal strategy, too, to allege this kind of rule breaking by the prosecutors. But the Baltimore County investigation had bumped up against a gazillion witnesses and all their defense lawyers and everyone those witnesses and those lawyers had talked to about the case. And so the chatter that reporters were picking up about the case just didn't, in fact, have to implicate anyone leaking from inside DOJ.

Nevertheless, Agnew's lawyers were pleased at the outcome. At least for the time being. They believed they had succeeded—for the moment—in pressuring the prosecutors and putting them on the defensive. This was a matter of perception, though. "Bullshit," says Tim Baker. "There wasn't any pressure about leaks," he says, because the Justice Department trusted that no one was leaking. "The pressure was get the guy out of the vice presidency. That was always the pressure."

The Baltimore team put their heads down and continued tying up the loose ends of their case. "That was noise," Ron Liebman says of the investigations into the leaks, "noise to be pushed aside. We knew that—that's all designed to distract you, don't let it distract you. We were too good for that.

"Kids that we were, we were too good for that."

Kids that they were, Baker and his two partners in Baltimore didn't know the half of it. The three young prosecutors had been entirely shielded from another, more insidious pressure campaign waged against the U.S. Attorney's Office for the District of Maryland. There was no paper trail on this campaign; it was hidden from public view. Hidden then and hidden for years after was the stunning fact that Agnew had been attempting, from the very beginning, to use the power of his office to obstruct the investigation or to shut it down entirely.

The scope of that secret effort would be a secret to the prosecutors it targeted, for years. For decades.

★ ★ ★

SPIRO AGNEW HAD received the first frantic phone call about an investigation in Baltimore County from his personal lawyer, George White, in early February 1973. He was away on official business, but the call from the attorney was urgent. "His voice was strained," Agnew later recalled of White, "and he sounded like a man under tremendous pressure. He said he had to speak to me immediately about a matter that was too dangerous to discuss over the telephone."

White had picked up indications that Agnew's old associates were being approached by federal prosecutors. Barney Skolnik, Tim Baker, and Ron Liebman were, at that moment, just beginning to document and unravel the Baltimore County kickback operation. When they had reached out to engineers like Lester Matz and Jerry Wolff, those men, in turn, called up George White in a full-on panic.

"Matz and Wolff were threatening to implicate me," Agnew recalled his lawyer telling him in a face-to-face meeting. "He expressed great fear that their threats could be extremely harmful to me." Despite the urgency of the situation, and the request from Matz and Wolff that he get involved, Agnew was firm in his response. "I said I could not stop the investigation and I would not do so if I had the power."

That's the story Agnew told for decades: when he learned about the investigation early that year, he just accepted the news and made no move to interfere. The records show that in fact he began taking action, almost immediately, to shut it down.

We know this—in large part—because there are tapes.

Hours and hours and hours of tapes, secretly recorded inside the White House. The recording system, installed in the Oval Office, the Cabinet Room, Camp David, and elsewhere, famously led to Nixon's political demise when conversations about the Watergate cover-up were released to the public. But those tapes also caught other conversations, including several about an unsettling little ongoing investigation in Maryland.

On top of the secret White House taping system, Nixon's trusted White House chief of staff, H. R. Haldeman, was making an entirely separate set of tapes that spring. Haldeman—*what was he thinking*—sat down every eve-

ning and narrated the day's events into a small voice re-
corder, creating a contemporaneous and growing audio
diary of his days at Nixon's right hand. Haldeman recounted White House happenings, important meetings,
conversations with the president. On the evening of April
10, 1973, he recorded his memory of this notable, and no-
tably unusual, meeting.

ADMINISTRATIVELY RESTRICTED

SCHEDULE FOR THE
VICE PRESIDENT OF THE UNITED STATES

TUESDAY, APRIL 10, 1973

8:30 a.m.	Bipartisan Leadership Meeting, Cabinet Room, The White House
10:00 a.m.	Appointment with Frank Deford, Sports Illustrated (EOB) (Thomson)
11:00 a.m.	Painting presentation by Manolis Galetakis (EOB) (Dunn)
11:15 a.m.	Appointment with Governor Tim Babcock (EOB) (Sohmer)
2:00 pm *Bob Halderman* 8:00 p.m.	White House Dinner in honor of Prime Minister and Mrs. Lee Kuan Yew of Singapore (BLACK TIE- LONG DRESS)

Agnew's schedule for April 10, 1973

HALDEMAN: The Vice President called me over today
and said he had a real problem, because Jerry Wolff,
who used to work for him back in Maryland, . . . is

about to be called by the United States Attorney who's busting open campaign contribution cases and kickbacks to contractors. It seems that Wolff kept verbatim records of meetings with the Vice President and others, back over the years, regarding fundraising, and he has a lot of quotes about how much we ought to get from a certain contractor, and so on, who has had good jobs.

Agnew knew that Jerry Wolff was a dangerous witness to him, maybe the most dangerous. If Agnew's former roads commissioner squealed to prosecutors, if he turned over the "verbatim" notes in his possession, he could reveal the whole sordid scheme. What Agnew wanted Haldeman to do—the reason he called him over that one afternoon in April 1973—was to help him stop the U.S. Attorney's office in Maryland from bringing Wolff in at all.

Agnew had already devised a plan aimed straight at the highest-ranking political appointee in the Department of Justice's offices in Baltimore. U.S. Attorney George Beall, Agnew knew, was a young, ambitious Nixon-appointed Republican whose brother Glenn, conveniently, happened to be one of Maryland's sitting senators. And, also convenient, Glenn Beall was a solid party man, a Nixon Republican through and through.

HALDEMAN: He made the point that George Beall—who's Glenn Beall's brother—is the U.S. Attorney there, and that if Glenn Beall would talk to him he could straighten it out. The Vice President's tried to get him to, but apparently not successfully, so he wanted me to talk to Glenn Beall—which, of course, I won't do—in order to verify a White House awareness and concern. He feels the publication of this stuff would finish the VP, because Wolff was with him for so long.

If you're ever trying to explain the concept of "obstruction of justice" to a second grader, this would be a good case study. The vice president believes that what this witness will say could "finish" him. And so Agnew tries to enlist the White House chief of staff to stop prosecutors from questioning that witness, by pressuring the lead prosecutor through his family. It is an overt, spelled-out effort to use political power and leverage to shut down a criminal case.

If this was a *failed* effort—if it had ended here, with Haldeman saying he wouldn't do it—then you could maybe chalk things up to the vice president blowing off steam. Having obstructionist *inclinations*.

But it did not stop at this conversation.

At that moment, it's worth remembering, H. R. Haldeman was neck-deep in scrutiny for his role in Watergate. And so, while he didn't agree to pressure Senator Glenn Beall himself, he did relay Agnew's request to another top White House aide. Three days later—on April 13—that aide, John Ehrlichman, brought Agnew's plan into the Oval Office.

JOHN EHRLICHMAN (ASSISTANT TO PRESIDENT NIXON): Did Bob [Haldeman] tell you about his meeting with Agnew?

H. R. Haldeman's notes from his April 10 meeting with
Vice President Agnew

PRESIDENT NIXON: No, I didn't see Bob [unintelligible]
what is it? He saw him?

EHRLICHMAN: Well, he saw him two or three days ago.
And your Vice President has problems of his own.

Richard Nixon initially misunderstands Ehrlichman,
assuming that Agnew's troubles must have something to

do with Watergate. But Ehrlichman quickly corrects him, bringing the boss up to speed on a whole new scandal approaching the White House.

NIXON: With this?

EHRLICHMAN: No, no, something else. . . . Back when he was Governor. Apparently there's an investigation going on in Maryland, and he asked Bob for help in turning it off.

"He asked Bob for help in turning it off."

Again, if it stopped right there—if Nixon, Ehrlichman, and Haldeman all said, *"Agnew is trying to get us to interfere with this ongoing investigation, but we obviously can't do that"*—then perhaps it would fall short of the legal definition of obstruction of justice. But it didn't. On June 14, with Lester Matz already cooperating with prosecutors and Jerry Wolff about to make a deal, Agnew himself was in the Oval Office running through the details of his plan with Richard Nixon and fuming to the president about this Nixon-appointed U.S. Attorney who was now causing Agnew so much heartburn.

VICE PRESIDENT SPIRO AGNEW: Can you imagine a guy going into, on an in-depth investigation, and going into the county that I was in and beginning this? Well, I'm getting all kinds of subtle information drifting back. They're trying to put the heat on me to try to interfere. I said, "I couldn't interfere if I wanted to. What do you want me to do, obstruct justice?" But what I'm afraid is going to happen: there are going to be some accusations leveled against me before this is over. Nothing that'll—that can stick in any fashion. But just the accusations now!

PRESIDENT RICHARD NIXON: What do you think they're going to do? I don't know. Look, I mean, what about— I'll frankly be quite candid. Who is the U.S. Attorney that's handling it? Is it Beall?

AGNEW: Beall.

NIXON: Is he a good boy? Why the hell did we appoint him?

As the conversation spools out, Nixon and Agnew begin to explore, er, options.

NIXON: Well, let's talk about what we can do. I don't want to just talk about what you've done.

AGNEW: Well—

NIXON: Let me say first, don't—as far as the line is concerned here—it's going to be hard-nosed. There isn't going to be anything to talk about. [mimicking critics] *"Well, we better get a special prosecutor, and we've got to look into this,"* and [unclear]. Balls! We've gone down that road [with Watergate]. We've made that mistake. No more.

AGNEW: Well, the way—

NIXON: The more you give them, the more they want.

AGNEW: The way this thing may come out, this—an engineer or somebody may accuse not only me, but the governor—

NIXON: Your predecessors.

AGNEW: —the governor, the county executive of Anne Arundel County, the mayor of Baltimore city. I mean, it may turn out to be—

NIXON: Accuse you of what?

AGNEW: Accuse me of—

NIXON: Putting the pressure on them to make contributions?

AGNEW: No, he may say he gave me a kickback of some kind. Came over here and handed me $50,000. Totally ridiculous. But—

NIXON: Oh, God.

AGNEW: I mean, they say it. I don't know what this guy's liable to say.

NIXON: And Ted, they're—

AGNEW: They say he gave a federal judge some money. There are all kinds of rumors.

NIXON: Good God, isn't it awful?

AGNEW: But this man is—

NIXON: Well, can we destroy him?

AGNEW: Well, I don't think there'll be much credence if he goes the whole way and says—and implicates every public official in the state of Maryland.

The man that Richard Nixon wonders about *"destroying"* is Lester Matz, who had been toting envelopes of cash for Agnew across the White House lawn, right under Nixon's nose.

Eventually, Nixon and Agnew agree they need to put some heat on U.S. Attorney George Beall. To shut the probe down before it reaches the vice president.

AGNEW: Here's the thing that needs to in some way—if he got it, [George] Beall can do it—somehow he's got to finish out what he's got on the burner.

NIXON: Who's this now?

AGNEW: Beall, the district attorney.

NIXON: Beall. Yeah.

AGNEW: He's got these cases. Now he has to finish them out. And get these damn—he's got 30 IRS people in there snooping around there. They're looking at everybody, every—

NIXON: But how can we get that word to him, though? You know—

AGNEW: We've gotten it to him.

NIXON: No, now, you haven't. See, Beall—George Beall—

AGNEW: George Beall.

NIXON: What about his—

AGNEW: Glenn Beall's the only way to influence this.

NIXON: The senator?

AGNEW: Yes. And Glenn's concerned because he got a pretty good contribution himself through the—

NIXON: Well, has Glenn Beall been talked to?

AGNEW: Yes.

NIXON: Who's this? This is [Glenn Beall's] son?

AGNEW: His brother.

NIXON: Brother? Ah, I see. Well, Glenn Beall better take a real deep, we helped him bury [his Democratic opponent] in '70. Bury him.

And there it is. Clear as a Beall.

Senator Beall, they believed, owed the White House a favor because Nixon and Agnew had helped him get elected three years earlier. George and Glenn Beall's father had lost his Senate seat in 1964; when it came up again in 1970, Nixon and Agnew personally helped Glenn avenge the loss by campaigning for him in Maryland, multiple times. And it worked: the Republican Party got that Senate seat back, and so did the Beall family.

Now one of the Beall sons was going to try to destroy Spiro Agnew with this investigation? *No.* Nixon and Agnew decided it was time for Glenn Beall to return the favor and lean on his little brother, the prosecutor.

"Glenn Beall's the only way to influence this," Agnew tells Nixon.

At this point, the two men have openly discussed their plan to shut down the prosecutors and to "destroy" a witness who might be particularly damaging. Then they go one step further.

Senator Glenn Beall, newly elected, reenacts his inauguration with Vice President Spiro Agnew.

AGNEW: Now, let me ask one other question.

NIXON: But, now, wait a minute. Don't leave this. What do we do with this?

AGNEW: Well, I don't think we can do anything at this point except somehow get Glenn Beall [to get] George Beall, the brother, to realize that he's—to get, go in there, finish up what he's doing—

NIXON: Indict someone. Just like we told that [Watergate] jury: [unclear] indict [Jeb] Magruder or whoever is guilty and get the hell out.

AGNEW: Get this thing over with and get this guy Skolnik, who's a Muskie volunteer, the hell out of this office.

End the investigation now, and fire the lead investigator, Barney Skolnik, while you're at it. *He's a Democrat.*

The first article of impeachment drawn up against Richard Nixon a little more than a year later would be "obstruction of justice" for his role in Watergate. But what these conversations reveal is Nixon and Agnew carrying on an obstruction effort—in a totally separate matter. And they weren't just *musing* about doing this. They actually did it.

Decades later Nixon wrote in his memoir, "In view of all the other problems and our strained relations with Capitol Hill, I did not see how we could do anything to help [Agnew]. In fact, the climate was such that anything we did to try to help might boomerang and be made to appear that we were trying to cover up for him." That was a lie. Richard Nixon is caught on tape; covering it up is *exactly* what he attempted to do.

And he enlisted a surprising deputy to execute the mission.

★ ★ ★

HALDEMAN HAD BEEN ignominiously removed from the chief of staff's office—an early casualty of Watergate—by the time Nixon and Agnew agreed on the plan to strong-arm George Beall. The man Nixon chose to replace Haldeman was General Alexander Haig, a four-star U.S. Army general who had sped through the White House ranks under the tutelage of Henry Kissinger. When Haig got tapped as chief of staff, one of the things he walked into immediately was a secret plan, already under discussion, to shut down the criminal probe of Nixon's number two. Haig turned out to be totally down with it. We know this, again, because there are tapes.

On June 19, less than a week after Nixon's conversation with Agnew about "destroying" a witness and strong-arming the prosecutor through his family, the president was in the Oval Office with his new chief of staff trying to figure out who exactly should approach Senator Glenn Beall about having a talk with his kid brother.

ALEXANDER HAIG (WHITE HOUSE CHIEF OF STAFF): I want to get Mel [Laird] to get Beall, Congressman Beall, to talk to his brother and say "you ought to sit in on these prosecutors you have intimidating everybody." Just to be sure that they're doing it straight and fair.

NIXON: The Vice President talked to you about it again? Does he think they're after him now?

HAIG: That's right, he talked to me yesterday.

NIXON: Well, I'll tell you, I think you better talk to Mel, I don't think I better—

HAIG: No, no, no!

NIXON: I can't have it put out that I was trying to fix the case.

HAIG: No, no, no, you cannot do this. But I want you to be aware . . .

Nixon's fingerprints could not be on this; he and Haig agreed on that point. But the question they had was, whose

could? Who could be trusted to deliver the message, and
deliver it with suitable discretion?

> HAIG: So, if [Glenn] Beall can get his brother—who's the
> U.S. Attorney—who we appointed, who's a Republican,
> but who's turned this thing over to two fanatical prose-
> cutors, but if he just sits in on them and supervises this
> [unclear]—
>
> NIXON: You think Mel [Laird] or [Bryce] Harlow is the
> better one to do this?
>
> HAIG: Well, Harlow is in St. Croix, unfortunately.
>
> NIXON: Oh.
>
> HAIG: Harlow would have been far better.
>
> NIXON: Well, I just don't think that Mel will deal with
> this, he's likely to bleed the thing out.
>
> HAIG: Yeah.
>
> NIXON: I think [Bill] Timmons better do it, because Tim-
> mons is discreet. He can kind of talk with him and say,
> "look, you know, don't embarrass the Vice President
> and this and that."
>
> HAIG: Yeah, all we're asking for is to be sure he injects
> himself into this, to be sure this is being done not as a
> witch hunt, but as objective.

The very next day, Haig reported back to Nixon that the
deed had been done. But the middleman he used was not
Mel Laird. It wasn't Bryce Harlow or even Bill Timmons.

HAIG: The Vice President has been very nervous, he called me three times here.

NIXON: I know, I know, and you decided to have Harlow try to, well he isn't here—

HAIG: He isn't here, so I did it through George Bush on the first run.

NIXON: That's good, that's good.

HAIG: And Beall, Senator Beall, wasn't as responsive as he might have been, although he's damn upset about it.

"I did it through George Bush on the first run."
Al Haig had turned to the chairman of the Republican National Committee: George Herbert Walker Bush. The future director of the Central Intelligence Agency; the future vice president of the United States; the future president.

This didn't ever stick to Bush, maybe because these audiotapes have just been collecting dust for the last four decades. But the documentation is clear: he was asked to take part in obstructing an ongoing investigation into the vice president, an obstruction organized and directed by the then president, Richard Nixon, to pressure the prosecutor through his family, using political leverage. And George H. W. Bush did it. He delivered the message to Senator Glenn Beall, who then relayed that pressure to his brother George.

George Beall donated his papers to Frostburg State University in Maryland. In those records is an official "memo to file" from July 1973, acknowledging the attempted intervention. "With respect to conversations with my brother Glenn," Beall writes, "the discussions were most superficial and very guarded. He occasionally mentioned to me the names of persons who had been to see him or who had called him with respect to the Baltimore County investigation. Names of persons that I remember him telling me about included Vice President Agnew, [the engineer] Allen Greene [sic] and George Bush. . . . The only specific information that he passed along to me that I can recall related to a complaint that he had heard from Bush to the effect that attorneys in this office were said to be harassing persons who had been questioned by us in the Baltimore County investigation."

There are a few amazing things to note here.

First, of course, is that a future president participated in what was likely a criminal scheme to obstruct justice. George H. W. Bush would be no stranger to scandal in his time: as Ronald Reagan's vice president, he would have a front-row seat to the Iran-Contra scandal that nearly crippled that presidency. Despite public insistence that he had absolutely no knowledge of an illegal arms sales to Iran, Bush's personal diaries later revealed, "I'm one of the few people that know fully the details" of the operation. Weeks before the end of his own presidency, Bush unexpectedly pardoned five Reagan administration officials who had been convicted of crimes related to Iran-Contra, including perjury and obstruction of justice. (He issued those controversial pardons in consultation with his attorney general at the time, William Barr.)

George Bush's actions around Iran-Contra did ultimately mar his legacy. And yet he was somehow able to escape scrutiny altogether for his role—nearly twenty years earlier—in an equally brazen White House–led effort to interfere with an ongoing criminal investigation of the vice president.

Aside from the surprising guest star, there's also the fact that Nixon, Agnew, Haig, and Bush would even *attempt* to carry this out when they did.

By June 1973, the Senate Watergate hearings were on TV every day. The cover-up was actively unraveling. Nixon had just fired his chief of staff, his White House counsel, his attorney general, his top domestic aide—all supposedly to scrub his White House of scandal. But right then, at the very same time, Nixon and Agnew were ripping open a whole new bag of potentially criminal dirty tricks.

Agnew himself, while not involved in the Watergate cover-up, had no problem getting his hands dirty when it came to saving himself. While Nixon and Haig went to great lengths to ensure their pressure on Beall's family was through intermediaries, Agnew just did it himself. Agnew personally lobbied Senator Beall over and over again. His notes and daily calendars, archived among his vice presidential papers, contain multiple face-to-face meetings in his office with Beall in the months before the investigation went public.

Perhaps the most remarkable revelation, though, is that the young prosecutors who were building their case that spring and summer—the case the president and the vice president were trying to shut down at the same time—have never known about any of this.

More than four decades later, this is all brand-new information to them.

During separate interviews, Barney Skolnik, Tim Baker, and Ron Liebman were provided transcripts of conversations they had never seen before: the Oval Office discussions involving Nixon, Haig, and Agnew, and the audio diary recorded by Haldeman.

"Oh, he had an audio diary? Jesus!" says Skolnik. "That's the kind of classic crap that we feared might happen," he says of the plan laid out on Haldeman's tapes. "Somebody like Agnew going to somebody like Haldeman to go to somebody like Glenn Beall. I mean, that's what our president calls 'the swamp.' I mean, that's the swamp in operation!" He adds that he and his colleagues had "no idea" any of this was going on.

When Ron Liebman sees the transcript of Nixon talking about "destroying" a witness in their case, he shakes his head. *"Well, can we destroy him?"* he repeats. "Forty-five years later, and my blood still boils when I read stuff like that.

"This is the Nixon White House. This is what they did across the board." What's on these tapes, the former federal prosecutor says, is "clearly obstruction of justice, or attempt to obstruct justice. Clearly." When asked if an obstruction of justice charge would have been on his mind had he known about these recordings at the time, he responds, "You bet, you bet."

Tim Baker is referenced directly in one of the conversations, as one of the "fanatical prosecutors" digging in places the Nixon White House did not want them to go.

When he reads this, Baker laughs out loud. "Two fanatical prosecutors!" he exclaims. "That's funny. Well, we were—I mean, fanatical?—boy, once we thought he was guilty, then we were really focused. We were gonna do this. We were gonna get this guy out of there and more."

And that moment on the White House tapes when Nixon and Agnew also talked about getting the lead prosecutor, Barney Skolnik, fired from the case? Skolnik himself never knew about that, either. When he reads Agnew's line "Get this thing over with and get this guy Skolnik, who's a Muskie volunteer, the hell out of this office," he erupts in surprise. "Oh, there's my name! Wow! Agnew said my name! Oh, joy." He stares at the words, going over them again and laughing under his breath. "Makes my whole life worthwhile." He repeats, *"Get him the hell out of this office."*

"This doesn't just make my day," he says, laughing, "this makes my decade."

Skolnik, not for nothing, also agrees with Liebman's legal assessment when it comes to the issue of obstruction. "This is essentially somebody under investigation going to an authority—in this case, happens to be the president—to say not just 'stop the investigation' but get a prosecutor *fired* for no apparent reason other than he's running the investigation. That's obviously illegal and obstruction of justice. And to have political pressure put on the lead prosecutor—George—to stop the investigation, again for no discernible reason." This wasn't "'Stop the investigation because statute of limitations is run' or, fill in the blank, some legitimate reason," Skolnik says. This was

"'Stop it because I want it stopped. Because I am exposed to possible criminal prosecution.' Obviously that's obstruction of justice. I mean, all of these conversations are, if not literally illegal, they are certainly suggesting that illegal things be done."

All three prosecutors, reading through the conversations for the first time, reveal that their emotions about this case are still very much on the surface. "It makes your skin crawl, doesn't it?" says Liebman. "It really makes your skin crawl. Even forty-five years later, with all the stuff that we have come across in terms of public corruption, it still makes your skin crawl."

There is a reason these three men never knew about any of these conversations. And it's because of a kind of heroism from their boss, George Beall.

The obstruction effort launched by Spiro Agnew and carried out by the whole machinery of the White House and Republican Party . . . that plan was executed as intended. It got to Senator Glenn Beall. Repeatedly. And Beall did, in fact, reach out to his little brother about it, repeatedly. George Beall wrote in his files that his brother "relate[d] to me . . . expression[s] of concern" he was getting from power brokers in Washington. The pressure to shut down the investigation reached its target.

But George Beall took the heat, all of it, and refused to stop.

He memorialized the attempt to influence him for the record, for history, but we now know that he never passed a word of it on to his team of public servants that was working around the clock to build the case. "George never once said anything like 'Hey, you know, my brother called and he says, this is really causing a problem, are we really sure about this?'" Liebman says. "Nothing like that ever, ever happened." If it had, Liebman continues, "there would have been the mutiny of mutinies on the part of Tim, Barney, and me. But it wouldn't have happened, because there's no way that our boss, George Beall, would come near that. One hundred percent."

"There wasn't any moment in which George hesitated at all about this," Baker concurs.

"Whatever they wanted George to do," Skolnik adds with amazement, "he didn't do!"

George Beall was all of thirty-five years old at the time. He was a Republican on the rise, with an entire career ahead of him. But he refused to bow to pressure coming right at him from this Republican White House, through his direct family. The efforts of Agnew, Nixon, Haldeman, Haig, George Bush, and others—they failed because Beall had an investigation to pursue, and he had independent public servants to protect and stand up for, and he never once blinked.

CHAPTER 9

"HIGH-RISK BALL"

Back in the summer of 1971, when Nixon was first starting to gear up for his reelection effort, he made a curious—and, in retrospect, telling—decision concerning the tasks and whereabouts of his vice president, Spiro Agnew. That July, the Nixon White House dispatched Vice President Agnew on a monthlong, eleven-nation diplomatic mission through Asia, Europe, the Middle East, and Africa. Agnew was to act as the administration's roving "goodwill ambassador," promoting American interests across the globe. The Vice Presidential World Tour would be good for Agnew, who still lacked for gravitas in international affairs, and thereby good for the Nixon administration and their prospects for reelection.

But this ambitious little vice presidential trip turned out to be a bumpy ride from start to finish. A raging monsoon washed out Agnew's scheduled visit with U.S. troops at the Korean DMZ. Morocco turned into a hastily abbreviated visit for "security reasons." That country's sovereign was still a bit shaky from a coup attempt a few weeks earlier. The Kuwait leg was marred by local newspaper articles suggesting the visit was intended only to aid Agnew and Nixon's reelection the following year and had little to do with helping Kuwait.

As bad as the press was on the ground in those foreign capitals, the coverage back home was even worse. "After viewing the adventure from every angle," one editorial snarked, "it is difficult to conceive that the trip is anything more than an attempt to pump up Mr. Agnew's image by making him look like a world statesman."

Richard Nixon was relatively calm about the whole thing. This was statesmanship with training wheels after all; he wasn't asking his vice president to make peace in Vietnam or open relations with China. But there was one aspect of Spiro Agnew's trip that really stuck in Richard Nixon's craw.

The golfing.

Spiro Agnew managed to turn his "goodwill world tour" into a taxpayer-funded taste test of the world's finest fairways—and all with the news cameras rolling. While Richard Nixon watched, in horror, back home.

There was Agnew's golf outing with the new president of South Korea. And another with Kenya's foreign minister. On arrival in Nairobi, reporters noted, Agnew "promptly took to the fairways for a round of golf." During his swing through Spain, the vice president made time for yet another round "less than an hour after his arrival." And even though he had limited time in Morocco—on the heels of the bloody attempted coup—he managed to squeeze in a round there, too. It was his seventh straight day slaloming from tee box to fairway to green to tee box, making Morocco, as the AP reported, "the fifth country of the ten he has visited so far in which Agnew has played golf." In Portugal, the eleventh and final country on his tour, Agnew dusted off the clubs again for a quick round with his new friend from back home in America, Frank Sinatra.

Nixon watched this play out on television, radio, and the newspapers, with a growing sense of rage. The golfing was "utter stupidity," he told Haldeman, and then picked up the phone and continued his venting at the secretary of state.

PRESIDENT NIXON: He played golf every damn day!

SECRETARY OF STATE WILLIAM ROGERS: Every day.

NIXON: Every day! Now, you know what I mean, every guy's got to judge his own, but he's brought a lot of this on himself. . . . Jesus, a week, a weekend here. And the thing is, Bob [Haldeman] was just saying that this kind of a reputation will never leave him.

ROGERS: It's awfully—

NIXON: Every time, every time now he goes out to play golf, they're going to notice it.

ROGERS: That's right.

NIXON: He could've played once or twice but, you know. You can always take it up, but I just don't know. It's just goddamn stupidity, particularly, Bill, when we were trying to help him by sending him on the trip. That's what irritates me.

Richard Nixon knew that Agnew was a crucial bridge to the conservative base of the Republican Party that had never entirely warmed to him. Spiro did a hell of a job there. Nixon gave him that. But even for an inveterate political animal like Nixon, this didn't really make up for this one overarching problem: Spiro Agnew was a *terrible* vice president.

And it wasn't just the golfing. It was, well, everything. Nixon had worked his ass off, all his life, and still it took him decades to climb to the top of the greasy pole of politics. And here was Agnew. Next in line to the presidency. Having done next to nothing to earn it. Nixon knew the responsibilities of the veep job; he'd served under Dwight Eisenhower for eight years. When he was vice president, he told his aides repeatedly, he would never *think* of acting

•

as Agnew did. The laziness. The entitlement. *The golfing.* If he had behaved that way, he once said, "Ike would have fired my ass."

Nixon was flat-out annoyed by his vice president, on the most basic level, day after day after day. The president cringed when Agnew spoke up in cabinet meetings. He sent aides to communicate messages rather than take the risk of a one-on-one with his veep. He just didn't like being around his brash vice president all that much.

Nixon was never very good at hiding his feelings, so Agnew was not confused about his standing in the White House. "I was never allowed to come close enough to participate with him directly in any decision," he later wrote. "Every time I went to see him and raised a subject for discussion, he would begin a rambling, time-consuming monologue. . . . He preferred keeping his decision-making within a very small group. I was not of the inner circle."

"Agnew was just there," says his aide David Keene about the relationship. "Agnew was a resource or somebody to be utilized when he could be, and ignored otherwise."

Barely halfway through his first term, Nixon called the White House counsel, John Dean, and presented him with a surprising question. Nixon's daughter was "doing a little paper" for school, the president said to the young attorney, and was wondering how exactly a U.S. president might go about nominating a new vice president if the sitting one was, uh, incapacitated or resigned. Just to pass it along, see. To his daughter. Nixon's question to Dean was suggestive of two circumstances that would help change the trajectory of American history in the very near term. Number one, Richard Nixon obviously lacked the ability to construct a convincing, or even plausible, cover story; and number two, he was *already* actively scheming for ways to dump Agnew from the vice presidency.

"[Nixon] enumerated some of [Agnew's] problems," Haldeman recorded into his audio diary after a strategy session with the president. "He's dogmatic, his hidebound prejudices, he's totally inflexible and that he sees things in minuscule terms. We then talked about what to do to get him out."

Nixon and his closest aides brainstormed ways to entice Agnew to quit. Money was probably the best bet. He was getting fond of "the fast crowd and the golf course and the pretty houses," Haldeman said. Maybe they could set him up in a high-paying corporate job. Maybe he could go run a TV network instead. "That would be great if we could get somebody to buy CBS and have Agnew run it," Nixon told Haldeman. So desperate was Nixon to be rid of Agnew that he even considered appointing him to the Supreme Court, just to move him out of the West Wing (technically speaking, Agnew was a lawyer—ha!). But even Nixon knew that was a nonstarter. "It would raise holy hell in the country and the Court," he conceded.

Nixon ultimately decided the best play was to marginalize his vice president, rather than force him out. That silent treatment protected Agnew in one important way: he was one of the few people in the upper echelons of the White House who could say, honestly, that he had absolutely no knowledge of Watergate. He was never close enough to the inner circle to be privy to the details of the operation, he always said, and nobody had reason to believe otherwise.

In fact, and in a Watergate-centric political universe, Agnew might easily have survived Watergate and become our nation's president after Nixon's demise. But it didn't work out that way. And, to give partial and grudging credit where partial and grudging credit is due, we ought to thank Richard Nixon for that.

Nixon wasn't much for relaxing, but in the last week of August 1973 he was at least trying. The president had the perfect place for the attempt—his own sprawling beachfront property in San Clemente, California. Styled the Western White House, the enclave was the finest home Richard Nixon had owned in his life. He had purchased it shortly after his inauguration in 1969 and seen it enormously upgraded in the four years since. There was a formidable new privacy wall ringing the entire compound; a bulletproof-glass screen between the swimming pool and the public beach; a bulletproof window in his redecorated home office, complete with expensive throw pillows; a private three-hole golf course; a lush new addition of poppies, columbine, primroses, geraniums, and roses on the grounds; a new gas furnace; a heater for the pool; a concrete path so the president could motor between the residence and his office in his golf cart; an updated projection room where the president could screen any film he wanted for friends and family (*Lawrence of Arabia, Please Don't Eat the Daisies,* and *Ivanhoe* were on tap that week); and a $621 ice maker, "to ensure the president was not using poisoned ice," the Secret Service explained. The chief of the White House mess reasoned the ice maker useful for reasons not altogether touching on national security. "The President does not like ice cubes with holes in them," he explained.

Richard Nixon did manage to get in some golf of his own and some beach time that week, but it was anything but relaxing. His presidency was coming apart at the seams, in a manner unimaginable just six months earlier. The Nixon-Agnew ticket had won a landslide reelection in 1972, with 61 percent of the popular vote and a stunning 520 of a possible 537 electoral votes. Not even Franklin Delano Roosevelt's massive victory in 1936 could match that. Nixon enjoyed approval ratings just north of 70 percent in the early weeks of his second term and, according to the assessment of *The New York Times*, "presided over what many believed to be the most powerful Presidency the nation had [ever] seen. He was exercising his war powers without advice from Congress or, in some instances, his own military and civilian aides. He was moving against Congress through control of the Treasury, deciding the amount and purpose of funds to be spent. He was moving to shape the Supreme Court after his own ideology by going to greater pains than other Presidents in appointing 'strict constructionist' members. He was seeking to control the Federal bureaucracy by concentrating more power in the White House and by moving only trusted advisers to key positions in the departments."

But by midsummer 1973, the ongoing, nationally televised Watergate investigation was eroding Nixon's once overwhelming strength. The polls said about two-thirds of the American citizenry now believed the president was involved in the Watergate cover-up.

Nixon tried hard to wriggle free from the growing opprobrium in a fifty-minute nationally televised press conference on his second morning in San Clemente. "Watergate is an episode that I deeply deplore," he said. "But that's water under the bridge. Let's go on now. The point that I make now is, that we are proceeding as best we know how to get all those guilty brought to justice. But now we must move on from Watergate to the business of the people."

It was clear that wasn't going to happen. The water under the bridge was rising, and perilously so. On the same day as the press conference, Nixon's defense counsel was in federal court battling Special Prosecutor Archibald Cox over Cox's insistence that Nixon release any White House tapes that might contain evidence pertinent to the criminal investigation. Nixon's attorney was arguing against, on the basis of executive privilege and national security. "Getting to the truth of Watergate is a goal of great worth," Nixon's lawyer told the judge in the hearing. "But there may well be times when there are other national interests that are more important than the fullest administration of criminal justice."

Special Prosecutor Cox respectfully disagreed: "There is not merely accusation but there is strong reason to believe that the integrity of the executive office has been corrupted—although the extent of the rot is not yet clear."

Ouch.

Following on the heels of that, over the course of a week, a series of damaging news stories seriously impinged on Nixon's attempts at relaxation. The comic stylings of *Please Don't Eat the Daisies* notwithstanding, Nixon ended up having a terrible, horrible, no good, very bad week.

First up were reports that added detail to an old story that the Nixon administration had wiretapped more than a dozen of its own government officials and four reporters—including Agnew's old speechwriter turned columnist William Safire—during the Paris peace talks. The authorizing signature on the seventeen wiretaps belonged to Nixon's former attorney general (and 1972 campaign chairman), John Mitchell. The wiretapping was a useful tool for plugging leaks, the Nixon team explained, and wiretapping was still more or less legal if properly authorized. But that just made it all the more fishy that Mitchell had denied any knowledge of the effort.

Mitchell was in the news again the next day, after his wife dished to a reporter on an entirely separate issue. John Mitchell had recently assured the Senate Watergate Committee that Nixon had no knowledge of the burglary or the cover-up. But after Nixon repeated that fiction at his San Clemente press conference, Mrs. Mitchell cried foul. She called the Western White House switchboard, but they wouldn't put her through to the president. So she called up the newswoman Helen Thomas and told her point-blank that Mr. Mitchell was protecting the president because he expected Nixon to pardon him. And that Nixon had lied to the press corps and the entire country. "Nixon was aware of the whole goddamned thing," said Mrs. Mitchell.

The next day, and maybe to change the subject, the White House released a statement from the Coopers & Lybrand accounting firm laying out the details of how two of Nixon's personal friends had helped him secure the necessary money to purchase both the San Clemente compound and another one in Biscayne Bay, Florida (the Southern White House). These purchases seemed beyond Nixon's personal financial capability, and reporters—and maybe even Special Prosecutor Archibald Cox—had been nosing around the transactions. The audit released by the White House was supposed to explain everything. The report did not satisfy the curious press or congressional investigators. And it did not put the matter "to rest once and for all," as the White House press office had said it hoped. Among other oddities noted by reporters: three former members of the firm conducting the audit had been unconditionally pardoned after being convicted of distributing false financial statements and mail fraud—pardoned by Richard Nixon. That was awkward.

Nixon, flustered and angry, was sure it was Archibald Cox and his team who leaked the information about the pardons to the press. "A viper sleeping in bed with us," Nixon would call Cox.

The capper of the week came on the morning of August 29, when Nixon got word that he had been bested in federal court, by none other than that viper, Archie Cox. Judge John Sirica sided with the special prosecutor's office that day and ruled that Nixon was obligated to turn over nine White House tapes to the court. Sirica dismissed Nixon's argument that the Constitution gave the office of the presidency total immunity from any criminal proceedings, and that it was the president's prerogative alone to exercise executive privilege and decide what material should be withheld. The judge disagreed. Sirica said that he needed to listen to the tapes and then decide for himself what material was privileged and what material could be turned over to the grand jury.

"In all candor," Sirica said in his ruling, "the court fails to perceive any reason for suspending the power of courts to get evidence and rule on questions of privilege in criminal matters simply because it is the President of the United States who holds the evidence."

Nixon knew what was on those tapes, and he wasn't going to permit his own appointed special prosecutor and a lowly district judge to pry them from his hands. The president "will not comply with the order," the White House announced, and said the president's attorneys intended to appeal the ruling all the way to the U.S. Supreme Court. Nixon knew how much was at stake. If he lost, if the Supreme Court found that a sitting president could be forced to comply with a criminal subpoena, he was in big, big, big trouble. He might not make it through his full second term.

So that is the relaxing and refreshing week Nixon had just had when Spiro Agnew called him and demanded a meeting, face-to-face, to talk about his own dire predicament. Oh, great. Bring it on.

Spiro Agnew was feeling the walls closing in, too. Those damn federal prosecutors in Baltimore had persuaded the grand jury to indict County Executive Dale Anderson on thirty-nine counts, including bribery, extortion, and conspiracy. A few of Agnew's own co-conspirators, including Jerry Wolff and Lester Matz, were even name checked in Anderson's indictment. And there were news reports that Agnew's own bag man, Bud Hammerman, was negotiating his own plea deal with the Baltimore prosecutors. Just imagine what he could have to say about the vice president.

Agnew's demand for a meeting with Nixon was, at least in part, an effort to force a show of solidarity. "I don't even contemplate the idea that the Vice President is considering resigning," an Agnew confidant told reporters, when the meeting with Nixon was set. "He intends to fight for the office to which he has twice been elected."

Just ten days earlier, President Nixon had made a public show of backing Spiro Agnew. "I had confidence in the integrity of the vice president when I selected him as vice president when very few knew him, as you may recall, back in 1968, knew him nationally," he told reporters. "My confidence in his integrity has not been shaken, and in fact it has been strengthened by his courageous conduct."

Nixon's bar for integrity was pretty low, especially where his vice president was concerned. "Ah, he said that, ah, that for years contractors, who did business with the state of Maryland, ah, contributed to, ah, expenses that the governor, or the county official, or what have you, might have," Nixon later told the interviewer David Frost. "I think that he felt that he was just part of a system that had been going on for years, ah, and, that it was accepted in the state that people who did business with the state would help the governor out with expenses that he couldn't take care out of his own salary. . . .

"Ah and, ah, that, ah, that was common practice. He said that as far as funds were concerned, ah, he never indicated to me that he had accepted funds while he was in the White House."

Nixon's belief in Agnew's integrity—or lack thereof—and his calculation of Agnew's political utility to him seemed to be independent considerations; never the twain shall meet. But by the end of August 1973 and that terrible week in San Clemente, Nixon had decided that he really, truly wanted Agnew to leave office without any further ado, to resign. Like now would be good. But Nixon did not like to do dirty work, so he was going to leave it to others to deliver that message. What Nixon did do at the two-hour meeting with Agnew in the Oval Office on September 1—and then for the ten days that followed—was take a reading on just how hard Agnew would fight to keep his office. And what Nixon discovered about that was kind of terrifying.

★ ★ ★

"EVERY CRIMINAL LAWYER knows that the first thing you do, if you can, is to avoid an indictment," says Marty London. London was a criminal defense attorney and a good one. And in early September 1973, he realized he was living a defense lawyer's dream, something that he had never before had in his career: a client who was, arguably, *unindictable* by virtue of the job he held.

London believed he could make the case that a formal criminal process could not touch his client, full stop. "We took the position that you couldn't indict Agnew because he was a sitting vice president," London says.

His reasoning was based on an untested theory that both the president and the vice president had blanket immunity from prosecution while serving in office. Among other things, the Agnew defense team was going to ask the courts to consider the practical, real-life consequences of convicting a vice president who hadn't been impeached first. "If you indict the sitting vice president and you convict him before impeachment, what's the result?" London argued. "I guess, since he would be charged with felonies, he could go to jail! Now you've got the vice president of the United States sitting in jail. Does he have Secret Service protection while he's in jail? And what happens if the president at some point is removed? . . . Now the vice president of the United States in jail is the *president of the United States* in jail! He's either the president of the United States in jail or he pardons himself!

"The impracticalities of indicting the vice president," London says, "seemed to us to be overwhelming and strongly indicated that the Founders could not have intended that."

Agnew's attorneys were preparing to argue that per Article I, Section 3 of the U.S. Constitution, a criminal indictment could be handed down only *after* a vice president had been impeached by the House and convicted by the Senate: "Judgment in Cases of Impeachment shall not extend further than to removal from Office, and disqualification to hold and enjoy any Office of honor, Trust or Profit under the United States: but the Party convicted shall nevertheless be liable and subject to Indictment, Trial, Judgment and Punishment, according to Law." There it was in black and white. Sort of. If you read it twice, backward, and maybe after a drink. Anyway, Agnew was ready to argue that all the way to the Supreme Court.

And as far-flung as that prospect might seem for a defense of a vice president, Marty London also knew this: that very question was already hanging fire in the federal courts. Nixon's attorneys had already made the same argument in the case of the White House tapes. The president of the United States was "not above the law," Nixon's legal team had argued in a ten-thousand-word brief, but he was not "liable to prosecution and punishment in the ordinary course of law for crimes he has committed, but only after he has been impeached, convicted and removed from office."

These were constitutional questions that had not yet been contemplated by the courts in 1973. A Supreme Court decision would be monumental . . . and binding. Here was Agnew pursuing his own self-interested rulings on these questions, without conferring with Nixon's own legal team. What if Agnew lost his arguments, and his case resolved in such a way that the court of final resort implied, or simply stated, that not only a vice president but a *president* could be brought up on criminal charges? It was not good timing, for Richard Nixon, for Agnew to be playing with that kind of fire in the Justice Department and in the federal courts.

By September 10, 1973, Nixon had heard enough. Agnew's scheming now posed an existential threat to his own presidential well-being. Nixon had also, by then, been read into the state of the investigation in Baltimore. Richardson was ready to present the evidence against Agnew to a grand jury, and the word on the street was that the prosecutors had a very strong case. So Nixon dispatched a number of aides, including his surly and hard-charging chief of staff, Al Haig, the man with the most menacing eyebrows in all of Washington, to give Agnew and his lawyers some advice. "The best solution, Nixon thought, was for Agnew to decide for himself that he must do the honorable thing and depart," Haig later wrote.

When Haig began to apply pressure, though, Agnew blew his top. He was being railroaded, he argued, by people who were not "fair-minded." And the president "was being emasculated by his own Attorney General."

Haig was having none of it. "You'll be playing high-risk ball," he warned Agnew, if his intention was to drag this out, "the president may not back you." Agnew remained insistent. There was no way he was willing to go down without a real fight. And besides, he still had some tricks up his sleeve he was eager to pull out.

Haig blew his own top, too. And came out with the blunt message he had been sent to deliver. It was time for the vice president to give it up and resign.

Agnew, true to character, refused.

"I'll fight this," he told Haig.

If the president wanted his resignation, he should come ask for it himself, and Agnew knew Nixon wouldn't. The president "did not have the stomach to confront me openly," he later wrote. "[He] resisted dealing with any personal crisis on a man-to-man basis."

Then again, Agnew had got the message loud and clear: he'd lost what little backing he had from the most important man in Washington.

CHAPTER 10

★ ★ ★

"TWO CONDITIONS"

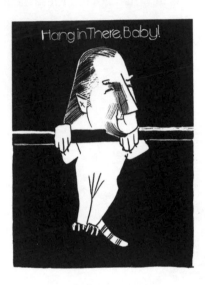

A ttorney General Elliot Richardson was not surprised when he got the call from Spiro Agnew's legal counsel, Jud Best. But he was relieved. The seriousness of the Agnew situation had been weighing on Richardson ever since George Beall and his prosecutors had visited themselves and their case on his office ten weeks earlier.

In the intervening months, the Watergate scandal had become a downhill locomotive with nobody manning the brakes. Archibald Cox appeared to be closing in on prying loose the White House tapes, which might just incriminate Nixon and might just force his removal from office. When that happened, according to Richardson's aide J. T. Smith, the attorney general knew "it was intolerable to have Agnew be in the line of succession to the president."

So when Agnew's legal team finally called Richardson and suggested that the vice president was ready to negotiate, the attorney general wasted no time in setting a first meeting. He could do it the next day. He was more than ready. He had been preparing for this, in a sense, his entire career.

Elliot Lee Richardson was awarded a Bronze Star and a Purple Heart for his distinguished service in World War II. Upon returning to the United States, he earned his law degree in 1947, clerked at the U.S. Supreme Court, then joined a premier Boston law firm, before President Eisenhower appointed him in 1959 to be U.S. Attorney for Massachusetts. Boston-born, Harvard educated, descendant of Puritan settlers, Richardson brought a streak of Boston Brahmin moralism and a stubborn sense of duty to the task. He dedicated his years as a U.S. Attorney to uncovering the entrenched corruption in his home state and prosecuting some of the most egregious and unapologetic offenders. Richardson once said about his time as U.S. Attorney, "I had turned over a log and exposed to the light a scurrying colony of unpleasant creatures whose only reaction was one of annoyance that I had been so crass as to disturb their settled way of life."

A decade after leaving that job, and just four months

into his tenure as America's top legal officer, he was now staring at an even more stomach-churning sight. Another log had been turned over, and the creatures stirring beneath were none other than the president and the vice president of the United States. Their scurrying was now spectacle for millions of Americans, the gossip of official Washington, the chatter on the Sunday morning news shows. But that was all just talk. Elliot Richardson was the person actually and officially charged to do something about it.

Under the cover of absolute secrecy, in the second week of September 1973, Richardson invited Agnew's legal team to the Department of Justice offices in Washington to begin talks. The attorney general believed he would be negotiating from a position of strength, at least on the merits of the case. The man Richardson had sent to review the work of the Baltimore prosecutors, Assistant Attorney General Henry Petersen, had reported back by then: The witnesses were credible. They were backed by plenty of documentary evidence. The prosecutors had been even-handed. The case was ironclad and ready to take to a grand jury.

The prosecutors had even begun to draw up the charges they were prepared to bring against Agnew. "We now believe that the following offenses have been committed," they wrote to Richardson in a confidential document:

1. conspiracy under the Hobbs Act, 18 U.S.C. 1951;
2. substantive violations of the Hobbs Act, 18 U.S.C. 1951;

3. conspiracy to violate the Travel Act, 18 U.S.C. § 371 and 1952;

4. interstate travel with intent to facilitate bribery and/or extortion, in violation of the Travel Act, 18 U.S.C. § 1952;

5. conspiracy to violate the federal bribery, graft, and conflict of interest statutes, 18 U.S.C. § 371 and 201 et seq.

6. substantive violations of the federal bribery, graft, and conflict of interest statutes, 18 U.S.C. 201 et seq. (see especially 18 U.S.C. §§ 201(c) and 201(g));

7. conspiracy to defraud the United States, 18 U.S.C. § 371;

8. In addition, there may be tax charges.

"Although at this point in the investigation it is difficult accurately to project the exact charges," they conceded, it was clear that a multi-count indictment was at hand.

And with that certainty understood by both sides, Richardson was prepared to play hardball, to threaten the vice president with the full weight of the law—with multiple felony charges including bribery and extortion, and a potential sentence upon conviction of decades in prison. But Richardson was also willing to offer a way out: the chance to trade the thing Agnew most wanted for the thing that Elliot Richardson most wanted; a one-time-only golden opportunity for Agnew to save his own skin. Agnew's public position was that he wouldn't give an inch, that he was prepared to fight by any means necessary. But he was about to get an offer that would be all but impossible to refuse for anyone facing those kinds of charges and that mountain of evidence. Even him.

"We are about to embark on the most momentous plea-bargaining in U.S. history," George Beall told Barney Skolnik, Tim Baker, and Ron Liebman on the day before the first preliminary meeting.

That meeting was uncomfortable on all fronts. "The office was so small," Marty London recalls, "that Elliot would be sitting up at his desk and the defense lawyers would be sitting opposite his desk, and the government lawyers would be sitting behind us because the room wasn't wide enough for people to gather in a circle."

Subsequent meetings, which had to accommodate Agnew's entire legal team, senior officials at Main Justice, and a contingent from Baltimore, were convened in the attorney general's enormous conference room. "The basketball court," as Agnew's lawyers came to call the room, was just as intimidating. Hanging on the wall, London recalls, were a series of Richardson's favorite plaques, one of which caught his eye. "It was just a Latin phrase," says London, "the translation of which was 'Grab them by the balls, and their hearts and minds will follow.'"

Things were bumpy at the start. At the very first and vaguely preliminary meeting, one of Agnew's attorneys made it known that Agnew was willing to hang his defense on the Constitution itself. According to his research, said Jay Topkis, a sitting vice president could not be indicted. Richardson answered that bluff with one of his own; he said that the Department of Justice's understanding was that a vice president *could* be indicted and prosecuted, even while in office.

In point of actual fact, however, Richardson wasn't certain. Weeks earlier, he had asked the head of the Office of Legal Counsel, the department that advises the attorney general on complex legal matters, to research that very question and give him a decision memo. The OLC had yet to deliver its judgment. But Agnew's legal team didn't need to know that, at least not yet, and Richardson's pushback against Topkis did manage to effect a standoff on the issue. They left that meeting with Topkis agreeing to share his own research on the matter. Soon. You know, when it was in shape.

Whatever rumination Agnew's defense team went through on that point of law, by the time they were next ready to meet, they were also ready to deal. Any contrivance that their client might not *really* be facing the threat of indictment evaporated.

According to George Beall's notes from the very next meeting—held in "the basketball court"—Marty London told those assembled that his client was ready to make a deal, "to avoid the 'embarrassment to himself and to the office of the Vice Presidency' which would come from a prolonged trial involving 'allegations of manifold wrongdoing.'" In fact, London said, the vice president was already prepared to offer his resignation. This offer, right off the bat, was a stunning development. But the devil, as ever, was in the details—in the *terms* of surrender, which Agnew's team carefully laid out.

"He would resign," Marty London says, "only if he could do so with no possibility of confinement and he could resign with dignity. Those were the two conditions: dignity and no confinement."

"Resign with dignity" did not have the same euphonic ring as "peace with honor," but at least the vice president's attorneys could attach specific conditions to the offer. First, that Agnew would not be forced to plead to a "bribery" charge; they preferred a "tax" charge. Second, that he would not be forced to plead "guilty" to anything; they suggested a plea of nolo contendere, or "no contest." And third, that the vice president would under no circumstances be "booked" like a common criminal. No fingerprints. No mug shot.

These specifics were each negotiable on the edges, but the final condition, the most important of all to Agnew, was nonnegotiable. There would be no prison sentence. Any hint of jail time would scuttle the deal. "We were not willing to agree to anything that involved a prison term," London says. "And that was a rock principle."

For Richardson, whose urgent and overriding objective was to get Agnew out of the line of succession, the defense's offer was music to his ears and on point. But the attorney general had been a young prosecutor himself not so very long ago, and the insistence on no prison time, he knew, would be a hard sell to George Beall and his hardworking team in Baltimore.

The three young prosecutors had worked for almost a full year building a slam-dunk case. To them, the idea of allowing Agnew to walk free, after what he had done, was sickening. "We were in the trenches," Ron Liebman says. "We're spending all of our time—day and night—pursuing this case. And in our mind as Assistant United States Attorneys, if we find evidence of criminal behavior, then our job is to prosecute it."

The Baltimore team wasn't blind to the *national interest;* crowbarring Agnew out of the White House would be a big win. But these young public servants were also aware of a higher principle—the foundational American principle that no one is above the law. Anyone else caught at the head of a long-running bribery and extortion criminal corruption racket could reasonably expect a long stretch in jail. They didn't think that Spiro Agnew should expect anything different just because he was vice president.

"What applied for me," says Barney Skolnik, "was what I saw as the very detrimental message that emanates from his not going to jail. People who do this shit go to jail. So why doesn't he? There's no good answer to that. The message if he doesn't go to jail is that if you're big enough, if you're powerful enough, you don't get treated like everybody else."

"Everybody seemed to want different things," Tim Baker says. "I wanted jail." He scoffs at the idea that a symbolic day behind bars would have sufficed. "No, no, no, no, no, no. A couple of years," he says. "That's what he deserved."

Baker was a proud native son of Baltimore, and he could not forgive Spiro Agnew. His corruption was magnitudes worse than that of the local Maryland politicians he had prosecuted to that point. "I never really disliked Dale

Anderson or [the county officials] Jesse Baggett or Joe
Alton. They were the banality of evil, in a way. Did they
really do a lot of damage? Not huge damage. The engineering firms that they took payoffs from, they're all competent. They did competent work. The wastewater treatment
plants didn't fall apart. The courthouse didn't fall down. . . .
But Agnew wasn't the banality of evil. Agnew was evil."

This was someone who had thought nothing of using
the second-highest office in the land to line his own pockets. Who had leveraged his ascension to leadership—
powered by bigoted, polarizing rhetoric—to scale up his
grift. "I thought he was a really bad man and he shouldn't
have ever been vice president," Baker says.

So the kids from Baltimore were pushing hard for the
punishment they believed Agnew deserved. The lawyers
for Agnew were happy to offer up his resignation, but a
prison sentence was a nonstarter. After a week of negotiations, they hadn't even reached agreement on what charge
the vice president would be willing to accept as a pretext
for resignation. Or on whether he would actually plead
guilty, or simply no contest.

Meanwhile, everyone in the room was aware of the
press of time. The president was engaged in his own intense legal battle over the order to give the White House
tapes to a federal judge. "You have to keep in mind that the
president was hanging on by his fingernails at this point,"
Marty London recalls. "The big problem was this is not
gonna end well for Nixon," says Tim Baker. "Everybody
was very conscious that we don't have unlimited time
here."

"We're all sitting around talking together about how to handle this grave constitutional crisis thing," says Barney Skolnik. "One guy in his fifties and a bunch of thirty-year-olds, sitting around talking about what to do for the country."

From left: Henry Petersen, Ron Liebman, Tim Baker, Barney Skolnik, Elliot Richardson, and George Beall, in the attorney general's office

"It was extremely emotional and heart wrenching," says Liebman, who recalls the scene inside the attorney general's conference room: "I remember the first time sitting across from a bust of Oliver Wendell Holmes and thinking to myself, 'What would he do?'" While the young guns held their hard-line position, the more senior Henry Petersen argued that leniency was the only reasonable solution.

"Henry Petersen was so angry at us, the three prosecutors, demanding jail time," Liebman says, "that he got out of his chair—and he had this way of shoving his hands under his belt. And he turned to Tim Baker."

"You just want him to be treated like anybody else. Like any person!" Petersen cried.

To which Baker responded, "You're damn right I do!"

"We went around and around and around," says Liebman.

Skolnik fights back tears recalling the pressure they were all under: "It was, without question, the most intense professional experience of my life."

At one point, the Baltimore trio threatened something close to a full-on rebellion if Agnew was spared fair punishment. After they suggested they wouldn't be able to publicly support such an outcome, the attorney general responded plainly, as Tim Baker recalls, "You all have to do what you do, and I'm going to do what I do."

Five days into the negotiations, with the deal still held up on the question of Agnew's ultimate punishment, Nixon and his team loosed a big barge and sent it downstream to bust up the logjam. Nixon had told Richardson that he was not going to block the Agnew investigation. But he offered that to the attorney general as a kind of bargaining chip. "Once we get his problem cleared up," Nixon told his attorney general, "we can get rid of Cox." Nixon would let the Justice Department kill off his vice president, but he'd expect the department to shut off its Watergate probe thereafter.

Nixon was a political realist, which meant he recognized Spiro Agnew as a problem requiring very careful handling. The vice president's alleged criminality notwithstanding, he remained wildly popular with Republicans across the country. Nixon was wary of any perception that he was sticking a knife in Spiro the Hero's back. Especially now, with Nixon in need of all the public support he could muster to fight off Watergate. His political operatives in the White House agreed! A strategy memo suggested Nixon take a position that "does not alienate Agnew supporters in the crucial period over the next several weeks."

"If it had gotten out that Richard Nixon had personally done this," says Agnew's aide David Keene, "you're talking about the base of the Republican Party [turning on him]. Nixon could not afford to let his base know that he'd sold this guy out when he's asking them to stick with him at a time when he's in real trouble."

Defending his ineffectual vice president hadn't been easy for Nixon in the best of times. As the crisis mounted, the relationship between the two men deteriorated to a level of dysfunction rarely seen in a modern White House. (Agnew, at one point, considered vacating his office space at the White House and moving down the street to the Senate.) Nixon's press operation took pains to keep the knowledge of the strained relationship within the family—at least until the third week of September 1973—when Nixon loosed the logjam-busting barge into the media stream. "Some high White House officials have been saying in conversations in the last few days that it might be best for the Vice President to resign and allow President Nixon to choose a new Vice President," was the lede of a September 19 story in *The New York Times*, front page, above the fold.

When asked by excited reporters at a press conference that day if the story was true, Nixon's spokesman added steam to the story. "Here's how it went," the NBC White House correspondent Tom Brokaw said, describing the scene on the *Nightly News* that evening. "Question: Is the vice president going to resign? Answer: 'I have no comment on the story that prompts your question.' Does the vice president enjoy the faith and confidence of the president? [Gerald] Warren's reply: 'I am in a position where I am no commenting the entire story.' Another reporter said some friends of the vice president are suggesting that your 'no comment' is a kiss of death, would you comment on that? Mr. Warren would not."

The vice president buttonholed Al Haig that day and demanded a face-to-face with Nixon. He got his meeting in the Oval the next day, and not much more. "You must do what is best for you and your family," Nixon told Agnew. And just in case he didn't understand the code, Nixon explained to Agnew that the best option would be to resign, plead to some small tax charge, and "end this whole miserable business."

So Nixon broke the jam, or so he must have thought. By Friday, September 21, Agnew appeared to his own attorneys to have accepted his fate. He had a reasonable offer from DOJ, and he would announce his resignation shortly.

The vice president could take some solace in the support he still enjoyed from the Republican base and their spear-carriers. "I don't give a damn if Agnew is as guilty as John Dillinger," the party icon Barry Goldwater said. "He's innocent until somebody has proven him guilty. And if we've reached a point in this country where we're guilty just because some newspaper or some lesser member of the Attorney General's office hints that we are, then we've come to the end of justice in this country." As far as Goldwater was concerned, his friend Spiro Agnew—his choice for the Republican presidential nomination in 1976—was getting "framed." And now federal prosecutors are "lesser members of the Attorney General's office"?

That same Friday two members of Congress showed up at the White House to deliver the season's strangest holiday greeting. It came in the form of an oversized card addressed to Vice President Agnew, signed by a hundred congressional Republicans. The image on the front was a cat clinging to a tree branch by its claws. The caption underneath read, "Hang In There, Baby."

But Agnew knew he couldn't hang on much longer. The deal Richardson was offering was probably as good as he was going to get. Agnew told his attorneys he just wanted to take the weekend to think about it. He'd likely sign the deal on Monday.

And then . . . the news got out. Front-page large-type headlines across the country that Saturday: "Agnew Is Reported in Plea-Bargaining"; "Agnew Reported to Be Bargaining for Lighter Charge"; "Agnew Reported Resigning as 'Plea Bargain.'" Jud Best denied it, to little avail. CBS News quoted Henry Petersen, the Justice Department official Richardson had assigned to review the case: "We've got the evidence. We've got it cold."

Agnew was incensed. This proved it. This was a witch hunt. These Democratic prosecutors and their conspirators in the press—all those folks he had called out and shamed, remember—they were out to embarrass him. To rub his nose in it. Well, Spiro Agnew wasn't going to give them the satisfaction. Agnew was not going to sign the deal. He wasn't going anywhere. "They'd have to dynamite him out of office," said an old Agnew hand, Vic Gold.

"I'm innocent," Agnew told his lawyers, "and the public perception must be that I'm innocent." He wasn't going to be some fraidy cat clinging to a tree branch, waiting to be rescued. Spiro Agnew was going on the offensive. He was going to fight this to the ugly, bitter end.

CHAPTER 11

IN HIS TIME OF GREATEST NEED

F rank Sinatra's politics were slippery. Born and raised in blue-collar Hoboken, New Jersey, just across the river from Manhattan, he began life as a true-blue Democrat. His mother, Dolly, was involved in local Democratic politics throughout his childhood, and once Sinatra became famous, he was linked to some of the party's most powerful figures: Franklin Roosevelt; Harry Truman; and, most famous of all, John Fitzgerald Kennedy. Kennedy was not just a contemporary of Frank's but a friend.

The night of his inauguration in 1961, JFK made a surprise appearance at a swanky D.C. party his pal Frank was hosting. Sinatra was "staggered" by the gesture. "I only wish my kids could have heard" the praise Kennedy had for him that night, Sinatra later said. During Kennedy's presidency, the two were close enough that eagle-eyed beachgoers often spotted the singer lounging aboard JFK's personal yacht, the *Marlin*.

But the glitzy friendship ultimately fizzled—by some accounts, due to Sinatra's suspected ties to the mob. In Kennedy's judgment, that particular kind of controversy made a continued public friendship with Sinatra too much of a political risk. Which meant Kennedy hadn't understood Sinatra at all. Friendship was bigger than politics. Friendship was about loyalty and constancy, in Sinatra's moral code. Even if a member of your pack had strayed or got himself in trouble, he was still a member of your pack and, as such, deserved unconditional support.

That's probably why Sinatra and Agnew—the lifelong Democrat and the firebrand Republican—clicked immediately during a chance meeting over the 1970 Thanksgiving holiday. A coupla proud and scrappy sons of European immigrants, both made good. "These were ethnic guys who had come up and put up with all of the things that you get," says Agnew's aide David Keene, who had a front-row seat to the budding relationship. "As far as both of them were concerned, they were the same guy. They liked each other, and they were loyal to each other."

"From the beginning it was one of those rare meshings of two personalities that create extremely close bonds," Agnew would later say. If the persistent rumors about Sinatra's mob ties were a concern to Jack Kennedy, Ted Agnew had no such qualms. "I had heard all this garbage that was being circulated about Frank," he later wrote. "I didn't believe a word of it."

When Agnew hit trouble of his own, his famous friend returned the favor, *Ocean's 11*–style. Cutting loose a pal in trouble was against the code. This was about loyalty. After Agnew received official notification that he was under federal criminal investigation, he retreated to Sinatra's home in Palm Springs to lick his wounds. Sinatra invited his personal lawyer, Mickey Rudin, to join them. Over the course of the crisis, Rudin would continue to be available to the vice president whenever Agnew wanted free legal advice. And when the vice president determined, at the end of September, that if he was going to war he was going to need a war chest, Sinatra started making calls to fill up Agnew's new legal defense fund. Sinatra's friends were willing to take the calls, of course, but they didn't necessarily share their friend's enthusiasm for the VP. "Look, we don't give a damn about Agnew," one friend told him, "but if you want some money, Frank, we'll give it to you." He was fricking Frank Sinatra. What are you going to do, say no?

"I met a lot of celebrities during my years in office," Agnew would say, "most of them fine people. . . . Francis Albert Sinatra, however, falls in a special bracket, a bracket of one."

While Agnew built up his war chest and drew up his battle plans, at the Justice Department those early hopes for a quick, clean resolution to the crisis started to falter. That expected and much-hoped-for agreement to settle the case did not arrive on Elliot Richardson's desk on the appointed day, Monday, September 24, 1973. And Agnew soon made clear that his signature on the proposed document would be forthcoming . . . right around the time hell froze over. But Attorney General Richardson did get another highly anticipated piece of paper that same day, one that would be very useful in the coming war with Agnew and his attorneys.

Richardson had asked the head of the Office of Legal Counsel several weeks earlier to consider the question of whether a sitting vice president could be indicted. The team at OLC, while taking care to provide objective, thoroughly researched, well-reasoned, and binding guidance to the Department of Justice, traveled slightly afield of the central question at hand. The final draft of the OLC memo, dated September 24, 1973, was titled "Amenability of the President, Vice President, and Other Civil Officers to Federal Criminal Prosecution While in Office."

The question was about Agnew, but the OLC lawyers took it upon themselves to give an answer that was about vice presidents, presidents, and even other civil officers. And that answer was edifying on two fronts at that precise moment. By reasoning that a president *could not* be indicted, the memo shielded Richard Nixon from federal criminal indictment or prosecution while he was in office. That same reasoning, though, would also shield Spiro

Agnew in the event that Watergate ended Nixon's presidency prematurely and Agnew ascended to the presidency himself. President Agnew, in the event, would enjoy immunity from indictment for all the years he held office—likely three years at the least, maybe seven if he won a second term. The statute of limitations would expire on every count the U.S. Attorney's office was ready to bring in Maryland. Agnew would skate.

The path to finding this presidential immunity was a tortured one for the Office of Legal Counsel. The text in the Constitution was vague, and arguable. "Judgment in Cases of Impeachment shall not extend further than to removal from Office, and disqualification to hold and enjoy any Office of honor, Trust or Profit under the United States: but the Party convicted shall nevertheless be liable and subject to Indictment, Trial, Judgment and Punishment, according to Law." That language from Article I, Section 3, Clause 7 clearly allowed for criminal prosecution *in addition to* impeachment for "the Party convicted." But what about an indictment in the absence of an impeachment? Clearly, a person can be indicted after being impeached and removed from office, but did you have to wait until after the impeachment to start a criminal proceeding? Could it be concurrent with an impeachment? Before? Constitutional text offered no definite or obvious answer.

The OLC trawled through nearly two hundred years of legal proceedings and commentaries to arrive at their answer. "The proper approach," the September 24 memo read, "is to find the proper balance between the normal functions of the courts and the special responsibilities and functions of the Presidency." The OLC considered and rejected the argument that a criminal trial of a president would be inescapably marred by politics and make it impossible to impanel an impartial jury. They thought that could be overcome. The president's authority over the attorney general, his "power to oversee prosecutions," and his power to pardon federal criminal crimes (maybe even his own?)—these were all of interest, but not dispositive; they did not weigh decisively in the OLC calculation.

The real crux of the matter, according to the OLC, was a question of modern practicalities. The president was a singular officer in American government. He was the one and only head of the executive branch. Nobody besides the president had the legal power to perform the myriad duties of the president. Moreover, the presidency had become a job of much greater scope and authority than the Founders could have anticipated. "During the past century the duties of the Presidency . . . have become so onerous that a President may not be able fully to discharge the powers and duties of his office if he had to defend a criminal prosecution," read the OLC memo. "This would suggest strongly that, in view of the unique aspects of the Office of the President, criminal proceedings against a President in office should not go beyond a point where they could result in so serious a physical interference with the President's performance of his official duties that it would amount to an incapacitation."

So, a little criminal proceeding against a president is okay? But not too much? What was the point of no return?

The OLC averred that that point arrived well before a president found himself in the dock and on trial; indictment alone could be debilitating. "To wound [a president] by a criminal proceeding is to hamstring the operation of the whole governmental apparatus, both in foreign and domestic affairs. . . . The spectacle of an indicted President still trying to serve as Chief Executive boggles the imagination," the memo read, the last statement being both bombastic and entirely without facts or examples to back it up. The authors continued this breathless warning several paragraphs later. "To be sure it is arguable that despite the foregoing analysis it would be possible to indict a President, but defer trial until he was out of office, without in the meantime unduly impeding the power to govern, and the symbolism on which so much of his real authority rests. Given the realities of modern politics and mass media, and the delicacy of the political relationships which surround the Presidency both foreign and domestic, there would be a Russian roulette aspect to the course of indicting the President but postponing trial, hoping in the meantime that the power to govern could survive."

The Office of Legal Counsel memorandum finally, on page 33 of 41, turned to Attorney General Richardson's actual question, the one about the vice president's amenability to federal criminal prosecution. This had been a knotty conundrum for the OLC's head, Robert Dixon, who specialized in voting rights and election laws, not constitutional theory. "His office dug through two hundred years of constitutional deliberations and opinions," says J. T. Smith, who was serving as executive assistant to

Attorney General Richardson at the time. "I think they ended up being in sort of a head-scratching place where the opinion could come out either pro-or-con criminal process for the vice president. And at that stage, one evening, I took a call from the late Robert Dixon, who said, do you have any idea how the attorney general wants this to turn out?"

Smith didn't issue any edicts on the phone call that night, but neither was his answer vague. He told Dixon that Attorney General Richardson, their boss, very much hoped the opinion would come out in favor of the position that you could indict a sitting vice president. Dixon and his team made it happen.

Had J. T. Smith told Dixon that the attorney general's wishes were to the contrary, presumably, that binding OLC legal opinion could just as easily have proclaimed the opposite conclusion. And the lack of real conviction showed in the reasoning. Over time, Dixon's memo—asserting that a vice president can be indicted but a president cannot—has become fairly momentous when it comes to defining the legal limitations of presidential scandal and crime. But honestly, the memo was . . . kind of a piece of work.

First, there was some history. Vice President Aaron Burr had served much of his last year in office under indictment in New York state and New Jersey, having illegally challenged Alexander Hamilton to a duel and having illegally offed him in said duel. So, you can extrapolate from that to show that a vice president certainly can still serve in office while under indictment; Burr did it, so that means it can be done. Does that mean it should be done? Eh, we'll get to that.

Next, there was the issue of whether we really need a vice president, anyway. In the OLC's fairly withering assessment, a vice president's duties were neither onerous, nor unique, nor even particularly useful. And here the memo got a bit catty. The OLC enumerated Agnew's various official duties as spelled out by statute, by executive order, or by the "reorganization plan" that reflected the modern responsibilities of the vice presidency as of the time of the Nixon administration. These duties included being a regent of the Smithsonian Institution and presiding over "certain meetings of the Institution in the absence of the President"; chairmanship of the National Council on Marine Resources and Engineering Development, the National Council on Indian Opportunity, and the President's Council on Youth Opportunity; membership in the National Security Council, the Cabinet Committee on Economic Policy, and the Domestic Council. He also had "immediate supervision" over the Office of Intergovernmental Relations, whatever that might be.

"The operation of none of these governmental entities would be jeopardized if the Vice President could not attend them," the memo stated. "Regarding such functions, the role of the Vice President can be analogized to that of a cabinet officer." Ouch.

The duties enumerated explicitly in the Constitution were not much in the veep's favor either. He presided over the Senate and voted in the case of a tie. That's it. Big deal.

The rock-bottom purpose of a vice president, according

to the OLC, was simple and blunt: "The principal responsibility of the Vice President is to be ready to serve as President or Acting President should the occasion arise." In
other words, a veep's job is to get ready, get set . . . and
then just sit there. And if that's all he's doing, perhaps the
country can spare him without too much loss or worry if it
turns out that the cause of justice requires his attendance
in court. And potentially in prison. "It appears as a general
proposition that his duty to stand and wait does not necessarily require his total immunity from criminal prosecution. If the Office of the Presidency was vacated while a
criminal proceeding was being conducted against the Vice
President, the process could be halted at once."

And while this makes sense rhetorically at the end of a
long string of insults against the vice presidency as an office and occupation, there is a bit of a hole (or maybe a
pretzel twist) in the logic. According to Dixon's OLC
memo, a president needed to be protected from indictment because criminal charges against him would so tarnish his authority and credibility as to create the impression
that he was unfit to carry out the duties of the office. The
country would be robbed of an effective president, and the
country needs one. But—according to the OLC—when it
comes to a vice president, prosecutors could go ahead and
tarnish away. A vice president, unlike a president, need not
remain fresh and untainted by criminal indictment. The
Department of Justice was free to dirty him up while he
stood and waited. Waited to become president. Where-
upon the OLC memo is silent as to why it is that a crimi-

nally indicted vice president could reasonably get sworn in and serve as president, when the OLC concedes that a president would be crippled in office by the same prosecutorial insult. Perhaps the idea was that the ascension to the office of the presidency would somehow wash away all alleged criminality?

In any case, there it was, somewhat inexplicable and not particularly logically compelling but nevertheless binding Department of Justice official policy, spelled out for the first time in American history: a sitting president was not subject to federal criminal indictment; a vice president was. It was a legal mishmash, really, bits and bobs pulled together based on what conclusion the attorney general said he wanted at the time. But with Dixon's memo, Richardson got it. He got his green light.

THE DAY AFTER he received OLC's opinion, Richardson and Henry Petersen, the head of the Justice Department's Criminal Division, met with Nixon at the White House to make an official report on the Agnew situation. The Department of Justice was ready to take the case to the grand jury in Baltimore, the two men explained to the president, to secure the indictment. "Petersen, in his very detached way and not in anger, ah, but in sorrow, said, ah, that, it was his professional judgment ah, that, ah, the charges first, were serious, and second, ah, that they could be and were going to be corroborated," Nixon later recalled. "I remember Richardson saying there were forty counts or something like that." Richardson and Petersen both told Nixon they would have to recommend a prison sentence for Agnew. Nixon said he wouldn't stop them.

After the meeting with Nixon, Richardson gave his eager prosecutors in Baltimore the formal okay they'd been waiting for: they could begin to present their evidence to the federal grand jury, to get the indictment. Then the attorney general informed Agnew's lawyers that the criminal charges were about to rain down. "Elliot Richardson called up Jay Topkis and me," Marty London recalls, "and he said, 'Fellas, discussions are over. We're gonna go ahead and present evidence to the grand jury.' We argued he couldn't and shouldn't, and he said, 'I'm gonna do it.'"

The obvious legal move for the vice president's team was to file a motion to halt the grand jury proceedings before they got started. But Agnew had something else in mind.

CHAPTER 12

★ ★ ★

"I'M A BIG TROPHY"

At a little after four o'clock on the afternoon of September 25, 1973, just a few hours after President Nixon had discussed the impending criminal indictment of Vice President Agnew with Attorney General Elliot Richardson and the chief of the Criminal Division at the Justice Department, Henry Petersen, Agnew himself marched up to Capitol Hill to open a new front in his war. Sporting a conservative dark gray suit and a blood-red tie, Agnew entered the office of House Speaker Carl Albert with a three-page letter in hand. It was the damnedest ask any Speaker had ever received. "I respectfully request that the House of Representatives undertake a full inquiry into the charges which have apparently been made against me," the letter read. "I shall, of course, cooperate fully. As I have said before, I have nothing to hide. . . . I am wholly at the disposal of the House." It was a formal request to be investigated by Congress. And impeached, if they saw fit.

The vice president didn't think he could get a "fair shake" in a Maryland courtroom, see. A "jury" of his actual peers, his political peers, would be more sympathetic to the vice president than the trial jury of regular old American citizens in a federal courthouse. Members of Congress, after all, knew how the game was played. "'All of those guys up there have done the same thing,'" Keene remembers Agnew saying. "'I just want them to look me in the face.'"

Agnew thought he was setting up a formidable skirmish line. Given his army of Republican support on Capitol Hill—*Hang in there, baby!*—the vice president judged the impeachment process his best chance at survival. Even if Democrats impeached him in the House, Agnew believed, enough Republicans would stick by him in the Senate that he would be able to escape conviction and removal from office. More important at that moment, if he could get Congress to take up impeachment, Agnew was pretty sure the Justice Department would feel forced to stand down on the criminal grand jury proceedings.

Speaker Albert was noncommittal when he met with

curious reporters after the hour-long meeting with Agnew. "Nothing's ruled out," the Speaker said, "nothing's ruled in."

Albert passed the letter on to Peter Rodino, chairman of the House Judiciary Committee, which would handle the impeachment inquiry. Rodino "read the letter," recalls David Keene, "and said, 'Go tell [Agnew] to fuck himself.'" There would be no impeachment, not while federal criminal proceedings were gearing up against the vice president. The House wasn't going to provide that kind of cover for Agnew.

The battle between Agnew and the Justice Department picked up speed after that; two days later, on September 27, 1973, the prosecutors Barney Skolnik, Tim Baker, and Ron Liebman presented the evidence of Agnew's misdeeds to a grand jury for the first time—seven hours' worth of witnesses able to provide direct evidence of the vice president's having committed criminal bribery and extortion. The day after, Agnew filed a motion for a protective order "prohibiting the grand jury from conducting any Investigation looking to possible indictment of applicant and from issuing any indictment, presentment or other charge or statement pertaining to applicant." Agnew's lawyers argued in their filing that "the Constitution forbids that the Vice President be indicted or tried in any criminal court. . . . In consequence, any investigation by the grand jury concerning applicant's activities will be in excess of the grand jury's jurisdiction and will constitute an abuse."

The motion paused the grand jury proceedings pending a ruling from the judge, but this cease-fire did not pertain across all theaters of war. Agnew did not pause his battle against the prosecutors; he began to rally his own troops—his own *best* troops. They were not who you might expect.

The Republican Party that sent Nixon and Agnew to the White House—twice—covered a remarkably wide ideological spectrum. It included the Barry Goldwater libertarian Republicans of the 1960s. It included young right-wingers who would later make up the Reagan Revolution. There were moderate and liberal Republicans like Nelson Rockefeller of New York. And southern whites who fled the Democratic Party over the passage of civil rights laws.

But none of those disparate ideological slivers could provide the energy and legwork it takes to really get stuff done in politics. Inside the party, everybody knew who the real activists, the real soldiers, were: *Republican women*.

Democrats had labor unions organizing on their behalf and mobilizing their working-class base across the country. Republicans were developing an equally devoted grass-roots network in the form of conservative women. "That's where the ground troops came from," says David Keene.

And right there on the calendar, already scheduled, September 29, 1973, was Vice President Spiro Agnew's keynote address to the annual convention of the National Federation of Republican Women. The perfect place to raise the rally cry. At the perfect time.

The convention was in Los Angeles, and Agnew took the opportunity to head west a day early, for an overnight visit with a trusted ally, Frank Sinatra. The two pals got in a game of golf at Sinatra's home course in Rancho Mirage, then repaired to his private residence a short walk from the seventeenth fairway. Over the course of a pasta dinner (the host made it himself!) and then late into the night, Sinatra's prodding riled Agnew up to the point where he was seeing red. This was no time to play defense. The vice president had to be on the attack.

At breakfast the next morning Agnew warned his aides he might travel a bit outside the remarks they had prepared for delivery to the Republican women's conference. He wanted to get a few things off his chest but promised to contain his rage. By the time he stepped onto his Air Force JetStar at the Palm Springs airport, Agnew had received word that the speech would be televised, live, to the entire nation, raising the stakes considerably for the embattled vice president.

As Agnew sped toward the National Federation of Republican Women conference that morning, the Convention Center in downtown Los Angeles was already electric. Not even mealy addresses by the party chairman, George H. W. Bush, and John Connally, rumored to be Nixon's choice to replace Agnew, could kill the buzz. Attendees told an NBC News correspondent on the floor that they intended to show Agnew that "they're supporting him in his time of greatest need."

The crowd's enthusiasm, noted another reporter, was surpassed only by its hostility for the media there to cover the event. "Some women approached newsmen ready for a fight," the reporter later wrote. "Several women took notes or tape-recorded the speech [themselves] so they could report on it when they returned [home]—a precaution in case the papers did not tell the entire story."

Agnew and his wife, Judy, walked into the convention hall just before his 10:00 a.m. Pacific Daylight Time speaking slot—early afternoon on the East Coast. The crowd greeted them with thunderous cheers and applause, waving their signs in front of the network TV cameras: SPIRO IS MY HERO and AGNEW FOR PRESIDENT. The sound system blared Agnew's "My Kind of Man" campaign jingle, which was almost drowned out by chants of "Fight, Agnew, fight! Fight, Agnew, fight!"

Spiro Agnew took the podium looking like a man rising to his full height, a man unbowed. "I don't know what it is about [Sinatra's place]," one of Agnew's aides told a reporter, "but it seems to charge him up." The vice president then unleashed a nationally televised tirade the likes of which had rarely been seen before in American politics.

"In the past several months, I've been living in purgatory," he began. "I have found myself the recipient of undefined, unclear, unattributed accusations that have surfaced in the largest and the most widely circulated organs of our communications media. I want to say at this point, clearly and unequivocally: I am innocent of the charges against me! I have not used my office, nor abused my public trust as county executive, as governor, or as vice president to enrich myself at the expense of my fellow Americans."

Agnew then walked the crowd through the many and splendored ways he had been unjustly wronged and slandered by the U.S. Department of Justice.

Federal prosecutors, he said, had been intentionally and illegally releasing details of their investigation. "Leaks have sprung in unprecedented quantities. And the resultant publication of distortions and half-truths has led to a cruel form of kangaroo trial in the media! The accusatory stories maliciously supplied by 'anonymous sources.'"

The source of all the damaging leaks was not only the U.S. Attorney's Office in Baltimore, Agnew claimed, but also officials at the top echelons of the DOJ. "It was not through my fault that this became a non-secret procedure, but through deliberately contrived actions of individuals in the prosecutorial system of the United States, and I regard those as outrageous and malicious." When those bad actors are revealed to have "abused their sacred trust and forsaken their professional standards," he continued, "then I will ask the president of the United States to summarily discharge those individuals!"

With the convention hall hanging on his every word, Agnew started naming names. "I say this to you," he told the rapt convention attendees, "the conduct of high individuals in the Department of Justice—particularly the conduct of the Chief of the Criminal Investigation Division of that department"—Henry Petersen—"is unprofessional and malicious and outrageous, if I am to believe what has been printed in the news magazines and said on the television networks of this country, and I have had no denial that that is the case."

Elliot Richardson's trusted deputy, Agnew continued, had "made some very severe mistakes, serious mistakes, in the handling of his job." Seizing on Petersen, Agnew launched into detail about his failures as a prosecutor. "He considers himself a career professional in a class by himself, but a recent examination of his record will show not only that he failed to get any of the information out about the true dimensions of the Watergate matter, but that he also—through ineptness and blunder—prevented the successful prosecution of high-crime figures." Because of these shortcomings, Petersen "needs me to reinstate his reputation as a tough and courageous and hard-nosed prosecutor. Well, I'm not going to fall down and be his victim, I assure you!

"Now, people will say to me 'Why? You don't make sense. Why should a Republican Department of Justice and a Republican prosecutor attempt to get you?' Well, I don't know all the answers, but I would say this: that individuals in the upper professional echelons of the Department of Justice have been severely stung by their ineptness in the prosecution of the Watergate case . . . and they are trying to recoup their reputation at my expense, I'm a big trophy!"

Even Richard Nixon, neck-deep in Watergate trouble, had not taken the extraordinary step of attacking his own Justice Department. Not in public. Not like this. But here was the vice president: accusing Justice Department officials of misconduct, accusing prosecutors of leaking information to the press, and naming his antagonists and alleged bad actors and pledging to purge them from the government.

Agnew finished his speech with another jaw-dropping assertion: "I want to make another thing so clear that it cannot be mistaken in the future. Because of these tactics which have been employed against me, because small and fearful men have been frightened into furnishing evidence against me—they have perjured themselves in many cases it's my understanding—I will not resign if indicted!"

The Republican women greeted this with nearly a full minute of uninterrupted, thunderous applause. Agnew repeated, "I will not resign if indicted!"

The crowd in the hall approached DEFCON-1-level frenzy as the Agnew speech rose to crescendo. "Yelling and waving anything they could get their hands on, the delegates surged forward to greet Mr. Agnew after his speech," *The New York Times* wrote of the scene, "and one woman expressed the sentiment that 'he was fabulous, fabulous, fabulous.'"

CHAPTER 13

★ ★ ★

SUBPOENA ENVY

Elliot Richardson put out a statement within hours of Agnew's blistering speech to the Republican women's conference. The attorney general was not going to let the vice president's ugly personal attacks on Justice Department officials go unanswered. He was going to stand up for his people. "The Vice President has singled out for criticism a career public servant constrained from defending himself," Richardson wrote, his disgust dripping from the page. Henry Petersen "is a distinguished government lawyer . . . greatly respected by his colleagues in law enforcement," Richardson wrote. And then dared Agnew to come after him instead. "As long as I hold the office of Attorney General of the United States," he wrote, "I shall assume full responsibility for the performance of official duties by my subordinates. And I shall remain committed to the standards of conduct and fairness which Americans have long cherished and which our legal system is intended to protect."

But even with Richardson's pushback, Agnew's attack was still powerful. He was successfully turning the public gaze from his own alleged (and well-documented) malfeasance to alleged malfeasance at the Department of Justice. All Agnew had to do was assert, without any real evidence, bad faith by the federal prosecutors. Could they be trusted? Were they out to get the vice president? Was this all a coup by partisans and plotters to overthrow the elected government? His attacks were so ruthless and the story line was so provocative it was just irresistible.

Agnew's team of attorneys, meanwhile, followed their client's lead, essentially unlocking the nuclear codes and pointing the warheads at every institution on the horizon.

The vice president's legal team had been saving string since the investigations into Agnew had first been publicly reported eight weeks earlier. Each new bombshell article contained very specific details of the case—details only those with intimate knowledge of the investigation could possibly know. Every new scoop was invariably attributed to "anonymous" or "informed" sources close to the investigation.

Marty London had built a file of all the articles that began with "High sources in the Justice Department have told us that . . . ," "High government officials report to us that . . . ," or any similar refrain.

"There was no question," London says, "that this was a very leaky investigation."

London and the Agnew legal team had already forced the Justice Department to run an internal investigation into its own conduct of the case, with Nixon's backing. The federal prosecutors and their bosses were expending valuable time answering FBI questions about leaks and executing sworn affidavits as to whom they had spoken with about any piece of the investigation.

And then, in the first days of October 1973, while Agnew spewed invective-laden cover fire, his lawyers pushed even harder. They would try to hit not only the prosecutors whom Agnew was attacking in his public speeches but also the press, which was by now hot on the trail of every new twist and turn in Agnew's case.

The plan was a bit radical, legally speaking. Agnew's attorneys had worked up a motion asking a federal judge to permit them—the defense team—to use the grand jury to conduct their own inquiry. They would ask for the authority to haul in news reporters and grill them, under oath, about their sources.

This kind of tactic would be seen by most objective observers as a naked ploy to divert attention away from their client's guilt, not to mention a serious affront to the established First Amendment rights of a free press. But not everybody would see it precisely that way. And count this as one enormous break for the Agnew defense: one of those people might just be the judge who was presiding over the curious case of alleged criminality by the vice president of the United States.

Walter E. Hoffman was not the natural choice for this assignment. The crimes in question had taken place in Washington, D.C., and Maryland, and Hoffman was serving a lifetime appointment on the federal bench in Virginia.

Judge Walter E. Hoffman

But when every federal judge in Maryland recused himself from the Agnew matter, the Republican appointee Walter "Beef" Hoffman was tasked to come over to the federal courthouse in Baltimore and step in. A six-foot, two-hundred-pound former football standout from New Jersey, he had been dealt plenty of high-profile cases in his twenty-year judgeship. And, not incidentally, along the way he had developed a significant measure of disdain for the American press corps.

The imposing judge famously once called a reporter into his chambers to read him the riot act. Over something that didn't seem particularly sinister. The reporter in question had botched Hoffman's nickname—referring to him as Pudge rather than Beef. "Truth is the best defense of libel," he warned the scribe.

Marty London and his fellow defense attorneys had already watched the sixty-six-year-old Hoffman lecture the grand jury in the Agnew case on the perils of believing anything they read in the papers. "It is because I have learned, over a period of twenty years as a judge and an additional twenty-three years as an attorney that the news media frequently are wholly or partially inaccurate," he told them, "that I must warn you to disregard totally any comments you have seen or heard from any source [in the press]."

Hoffman noted to the jury, by way of a pro bono civics lesson, that "we are rapidly approaching the day" of a full-scale confrontation between "the news media—operating as they do under freedom of speech and freedom of the press—and the judicial system, charged with protecting the rights of persons under investigation."

Little wonder Agnew's attorneys suspected Hoffman might make for an easy mark. And they struck.

On October 3, 1973, at a conference the judge had convened with both legal teams, London loudly protested the unholy alliance between the prosecutors and the press. The resulting nonstop leaks, he argued, were unfairly prejudicing the public against his client, and they needed to be rooted out.

Hoffman agreed that leaks were a problem, but he wanted to know how London could be so sure of who the guilty party was. "They say that they're getting the information from the government," Hoffman said of the reporters, but "the government says, 'No, they're not.' . . . How do I know what [the reporters] say is true?"

"We considered that to be a big fat meatball right down the center of the plate," London remembers. "I reached into my briefcase and pulled out an order that I had written the day before. And I said, 'Here's an order; all you gotta do is sign it.'"

The document London presented would allow the defense to send subpoenas to the reporters of their choice, to force those reporters to testify about their sources—in court, under penalty of perjury. The defense would also be given license to depose the highest officials in the Justice Department, up to and including Elliot Richardson himself: to question them, under oath, about whether they were leaking.

The prosecutors were stunned by the move. "George Beall, I think he almost had a coronary," London says. "He was a young fella; I was afraid for his health. He got red in the face; they said, 'This is outrageous.' They said, 'This has never been done before, there's no rule permitting this, there's no precedent for this, it's just not right.'"

Hoffman was unmoved by Beall's protests. "The judge said, 'Where do I sign?'" London says. "And he signed the document. And that's really, to use a legal expression, that's when the shit hit the fan."

London was aware he was stepping into a constitutional minefield on the limits of the First Amendment. But, frankly, that was a side issue for him. "I was a lawyer here! I'm not a judge, and I'm not a philosopher-king," says London. "In this case, it was in my interest to get as much information from [each] journalist as I could, and I was willing to do what I needed to do in terms of legal process to get that information."

Agnew's defense attorneys, leaving court after winning the authority to subpoena news reporters and depose DOJ officials over press leaks. *From left:* Jay Topkis, Judah Best, and Marty London

A raft of subpoenas soon went out to *The New York Times, The Washington Post,* NBC News, *Time, Newsweek*—the biggest news outlets in the country. Agnew's lawyers had selected nine reporters in all. To London's delight, Judge Hoffman had not only signed their order to bring the reporters in; he also agreed to preside over the questioning to speed up the process, in the event that one journalist or another refused to cooperate.

"I knew what was going to happen," London says. "These guys were gonna get on there, and they were gonna say, 'Your Honor, I refuse to testify!' And the judge would say, 'Well, what's your name?' They'd give him his name and he'd say, 'Did you write this article?' He'd say, 'I refuse to answer that question.' *'Take him away!'* I mean, he would have sent every one of those guys—properly so—to the lockup. Obstruction of justice. And there's not a court in the land that would've held otherwise."

The press was blindsided and then quickly "up in arms," as London says. "They had fashioned lapel buttons, you know, it said, 'Free the Agnew Nine,' because [the nine reporters] all swore they would go to jail before they would testify."

While the news organizations deemed the subpoenas a dangerous infringement on freedom of the press, a few individual journalists had unexpected reactions. "I get a call from a reporter from a local New York newspaper who says, 'Marty, I'm in deep shit here, you killed me,'" London recalls. "'What did I do?' He said, 'I didn't get a subpoena!' We had at that time what was known as subpoena envy; everybody wanted a subpoena. I said, 'Well, look, I apologize, no hard feelings, I only served subpoenas on people who wrote stories that said they had sources.' And he said, 'I did that! I did that!' I said, 'Send me your article, and I'll send you a subpoena.' So he sent me the article and I sent him a subpoena, and the 'Free the Agnew Nine' became 'Free the Agnew Ten.'"

The Washington Post, whose main reporter on the case was one of those called to testify, developed a creative ploy to defy the subpoena. The reporter turned over all of his notes to the *Post*'s publisher, Katharine Graham, arguing that if a judge wanted to hold the paper in contempt, he would have to throw Ms. Graham herself in jail. "Let's see if [Judge Hoffman] has the balls to put Kay Graham in the clink," said a *Post* lawyer.

The NBC News reporter Ron Nessen also received a subpoena. But that evening, the network announced that he, like all of the other reporters, was "not going to disclose his sources, and he bases that on the principle of confidentiality, which is essential to the practice of journalism in a free society." To do otherwise, the president of NBC News said, "undermines the public's constitutional right to a free flow of information."

It was all a bit of a circus, but that was by design. The Justice Department was suddenly in the position of defending itself in court, and the press corps was now (rightfully) obsessed over the subpoenas served on their brethren. "Whether or not [Agnew's] lawyers learn much about [the leaks]," the veteran journalist David Brinkley said, "they will have succeeded, to some extent, in turning the public's attention away from their client and turning the attention and some abuse on the press." They wanted a distraction, and a distraction was what they got. And from then until the shocking surprise ending of the Agnew crisis, this fight over reporters' sources and alleged leaks from prosecutors was most of what the public knew about the status of the case.

But behind the scenes, away from all the deliberate chaos and upset stirred up by Agnew's defense, things took a dark turn for him right around this same time. On October 5, 1973, two days after the judge signed on to Agnew's plan to investigate the leakers, the court received an official filing from an as-yet-unheard-from Department of Justice official. Solicitor General Robert H. Bork, tasked by President Nixon personally, produced a "Memorandum for the United States Concerning the Vice President's Claim of Constitutional Immunity." This legal filing was basically drawn from Dixon's OLC memo about the indictability of federal officials, but it was prettied up by the authorship of the department's resident constitutional scholar, Robert Bork, and offered to the court as the government's official position on the Agnew problem.

Bork's filing argued that the federal grand jury in Baltimore should be allowed to get on with the business of investigating Spiro Agnew and indicting him if the evidence demanded it. The memo took pains to note that though the president was immune from indictment or prosecution while in office, the vice president enjoyed no similar privilege. Bork was not as dismissive of Agnew's enumerated duties as the OLC memo had been, but he was direct in his assertions that the crux of Agnew's argument was "without foundation in history or logic. . . . There have been many occasions in our history when the nation lacked a Vice President, and yet suffered no ill consequences. And at least one Vice President successfully fulfilled the responsibilities of his office while under indictment in two states. There is in fact no comparison between the importance of the Presidency and the Vice-Presidency."

At that very moment, Agnew's legal team was arguing in court that Justice Department prosecutors and officials were themselves the criminals for the way they were pursuing Agnew and that they shouldn't be allowed to pursue him at all, because being vice president made Agnew immune from prosecution. But now this filing from the solicitor general, on Nixon's orders, that no, you cannot prosecute Nixon, but feel free to fire away at Agnew!—this new official position of the government on the Agnew matter just cut Agnew's legs out from under him.

And, seeing it, Agnew's attorneys had to know where the court would come down. He would almost certainly be indicted, probably within a matter of weeks.

Richardson was not that surprised to get the call from Agnew's attorneys the next day. They were ready to reopen negotiations.

CHAPTER 14

★ ★ ★

"WE'RE GOING TO BE CRITICIZED FOR WHAT WE DO HERE TODAY"

It would be Henry Petersen who took the lead for the Justice Department in the final, fraught negotiations over Agnew's fate. Somewhat oddly, though, the judge overseeing Agnew's case also insisted on being there himself. Judge Walter Hoffman not only wanted to oversee the parlay session in person; he directed all the logistics. He told the lawyers on both sides to assemble at a location he thought reporters would never suspect: a single room, in a random motel, in suburban Virginia. The judge had checked in ahead of time, along with his wife. He instructed the legal teams from both sides to meet him in his room.

"Nobody in the press knows about this. This is a secret!" Marty London and his colleagues were told by the judge. "We were given specific instructions: 'If when you get to this motel, you see the press, you don't go in, you call me! Here's the number of my motel room.'"

When London pulled up to the Old Colony Motel in Alexandria, Virginia, that afternoon, he saw a crowd of reporters swarming the parking lot. "We tell the taxicab driver, 'Don't turn in, keep going, take us to the nearest gas station,' where we go to a pay phone and we call the judge and say, 'Your parking lot is chockablock full of reporters.' And he is pissed." So much for the stealth plan. Judge Hoffman told the defense lawyers to come ahead to the motel anyway, because the team from the Justice Department was already there.

And so reopened the low-rent, high-stakes negotiation into the fate of the vice president. "[Judge Hoffman] didn't reserve a conference room," London says. "This was an inexpensive motel bedroom! And the room is twin beds! And we're sitting on the inside of one bed, and Henry Petersen and George Beall and another assistant are sitting on the other bed, they're looking at each other, and down at the end—between the two beds—is sitting the judge in a desk chair. And we're negotiating what we can. It was a very awkward circumstance. When we wanted to caucus, the judge said, 'Well, why don't you guys go in the bathroom?'

"We resolved what we could," London says. But the two sides hadn't yet met in the middle.

When that not-so-secret roadside motel conference ended, the key and crucial sticking point remained unresolved: whether the vice president of the United States would be locked up. Both sides were dug in, London remembers: "They said, 'Look, we have informants who say that they gave money, and they have already pleaded guilty to felonies. How could we let your guy off with a plea to a misdemeanor when those guys who are cooperating are gonna go to jail for felonies?' And we said, 'Those guys aren't the vice president of the United States.' It's hard to argue with that proposition."

When Petersen and the prosecution team reported back to Richardson, the attorney general was nearing the end of his tether. This was the first week of October. President Nixon was under enormous emotional and physical strain. He was teetering on the edge of his own criminal liability regarding Watergate, as well as dealing with the brand-new brawl—the Yom Kippur War—that had erupted in the Middle East. And Spiro Agnew was still a heartbeat away from the presidency.

The attorney general summoned the prosecutors from Baltimore to a private meeting and told them it was time to think seriously about trading Agnew's resignation for his freedom. Skolnik and Baker clapped back. Agnew was a thief, and he deserved to go to prison. They wanted their bosses to press harder. Henry Petersen finally blew. "This man is the goddamn vice president of the United States," he told the prosecutors. "What do you want to do? Make him crawl on his belly?"

The Baltimore team finally started to back away from their hard-line stance, but they had a condition. They weren't going to stand up and offer the deal in open court. Richardson himself would have to go before the judge and the American public. Richardson said he was willing to do that. He was willing to take the heat, personally, from all sides.

"He was as disgusted as we were that here's another crook," Ron Liebman says of Richardson. "He was disgusted by that. But he also knew—more so because of his experience and his age than we did, I think—that resignation was more important in the context of the time than any of the other considerations."

"Attorney General Richardson was persuaded that the good of the country required that the vice president be removed from the line of succession," George Beall later recalled. "President Nixon was disabled. It was entirely likely he would not survive his term. It was intolerable and unacceptable for the Attorney General to have a vice president who was facing criminal indictment be in the line of succession."

"It had to do with the country," Barney Skolnik says. "It had to do with the top-priority importance to the country of getting him out of the vice presidency. That the country *must* have him out of the vice presidency."

It was a heck of a controversial decision, though. Years

and years of brazen corruption, including taking bribes and shaking people down—even from inside the White House!—all essentially overlooked. But Richardson made that call, knowing it would be unpopular not only with a large segment of the American public but with the principled young deputies on his team whom he had come to trust and respect deeply.

"I had sat around that table on four or five separate occasions over a period of a couple of months," Skolnik says, "and I had waxed eloquent about equal treatment under the law and how, as a matter of grand principle, I was standing in opposition to us sending a message that if you do this kind of stuff, you go to jail unless you're big and powerful. Because I had this role in all of that; it was very hard for me to ultimately say, 'I think he's right.'

"But," Skolnik says, "there came a point at which I thought he was right."

After he had wrangled his own prosecutors into line, Richardson called Agnew's attorneys into his conference room at the Justice Department for a separate meeting. The attorney general finally told them what they wanted to hear. The government was willing to formally endorse a plea deal with no prison time. "Okay, I bite the bullet," Marty London recalls him saying. "This is the only way it's gonna happen."

With the preliminary deal now agreed to by both sides, it was time for Judge Hoffman to review it. "The judge—who usually speaks in very direct sentences—makes a speech," London says. "We're going to be criticized for what we do here today, I know that," he recalls Hoffman saying. "But as long as the public is aware of what's involved and how we came about this, I agree with the government and with the accused's lawyers—that [this is] truly in the national interest."

And with that, the deal was done, struck on the afternoon of October 9. "The Agnew case is over; we'll do it tomorrow," Judge Hoffman declared. The vice president, he said, would need to report to court in Baltimore the next afternoon to deliver his plea and resign his office.

Marty London was not surprised by the lightning-quick schedule. Time was of the essence. "You don't wait," says London, a veteran of many high-profile cases. "Just because you have a deal now doesn't mean you're gonna have a deal in three days. You let three days go by, man, the leaks come in and the boat gets lower and lower in the water, and then it turns turtle. So, if you have a deal now . . . you do it!"

The vice president told his attorneys he would be there at the appointed hour, to make the plea. But nobody, including the attorneys, was sure the volatile Agnew would keep his word. And the next twenty-four hours were a down-to-the-last-minute, sirens-wailing sweat-fest like you almost can't believe.

In all of U.S. history, a vice president had never been forced to resign his office, which meant that the proper protocol for such an event was not altogether clear. Prosecutors dug through the archives to find a 1792 law that specified the instrument of vice presidential resignation: a letter submitted to the secretary of state. The prosecutors informed Agnew's attorneys of this discovery, but they couldn't write it for them. So Marty London and the rest of Agnew's defense team rushed back to Agnew's office at the White House to draft that letter.

"We've got two hours," London recalls. "I don't know how so many people got in that room." He and his colleagues found Agnew's office jam-packed with more lawyers than they could count. "Some guy who was, like, counselor to the vice president, another guy was there, another guy was there. Frank Sinatra had sent a lawyer!" And of course everybody in the room, London recalls, seemed to have his own idea about what the resignation letter should say.

"[One] guy writes a letter, 'I'm resigning because the press wanted me gone,' and the other guy said, 'The Department of Justice wanted me gone,' another guy said, 'It's the fucking Democrats, they want me gone'! You know it's everything. And we're going nowhere! It's an hour and a half later, the clock is ticking, the temperature in the room is eighty-five degrees." London finally jumped in himself. "I said, 'I got it, guys, I got it.'"

His suggestion was to the point. "I say, 'I hereby resign as Vice President of the United States. Respectfully.' Everybody says, 'Well, jeez, that'll do it.'"

The chaos in the vice president's office was nothing, though, compared with what was happening in the U.S. Attorney's office in Baltimore.

Agnew was going to be charged with only a single count of tax evasion—to which he would plead no contest—but the Baltimore prosecutors had argued for another way to inform the American public of the extraordinary breadth of his criminal activity. The plea deal allowed them to submit a detailed statement of evidence into the record, laying out exactly what crimes Agnew had committed. The payoffs as governor, the payoffs as vice president, everything they had.

They would ultimately draft a forty-page statement of evidence. But the day the plea agreement was made, it wasn't done yet. So the three Baltimore prosecutors stayed up all night to try to finish it in time.

"It was all written the night before we went to court," says Barney Skolnik. "It was like this all-nighter thing, like it was being back in college. We were exchanging drafts. I think maybe Timmy wrote, you know, these parts, and I wrote some parts, and Ron wrote some parts."

"We just started dictating. And drafts would go, pages would go," recalls Tim Baker. "It wasn't like complete drafts—sections would go back and forth, back and forth, marked up, retyped, marked up, retyped. We were on a deadline!"

Elliot Richardson planned to drive to Baltimore in the middle of the night to read what the prosecutors were putting together. "This is the attorney general of the United States at two in the morning in Baltimore," Ron Liebman says. "You know, on my best days, I wouldn't want to be in Baltimore at two in the morning!"

When Richardson arrived, he dove right in. "He sits down at George's desk and reads it," Tim Baker says, "and is very complimentary about it." At around 6:00 a.m. the team handed this forty-page statement off to U.S. marshals, "who then, we were later told, were doing in excess of eighty-five miles an hour on the Baltimore-Washington Expressway. It had to be to Agnew's lawyers by something like 8:00 a.m. in Washington, some terrible hour, and they got it there just in time."

They got it there, in fact, five minutes late. It had been rushed to D.C. with a sirens-wailing police escort as if it were the holy grail—which for these prosecutors, it sort of was. Read the document today and you will see the nicks and dents of the furious all-nighter: some questionable grammar and unfortunate misspellings; a dropped word here, an extra word there; missing punctuation. But those meager imperfections stand today as a badge of honor for those federal prosecutors—unavoidable scars from their headlong effort to head off Agnew at the pass.

Spiro Agnew was about to walk into federal court and plead to a tiny fraction of what he'd actually done, but these Baltimore prosecutors stood ready to enter into the public record (forever and for good) a remarkably detailed and cogent recitation of the *entirety* of the vice president's spectacular betrayal of the public trust. "[It was] absolutely necessary that the whole case be laid out so that the people, so that the country could see this wasn't a 'witch hunt'—to use a current expression—that there was a very substantial, solid case against him," says Baker. "It had to bury him."

"It was a big issue for all of us," Liebman says. "For the vice president to plead to a tax count and then to walk out and say, 'This is nothing. This is some little mistake I made. These guys are liars. I made a little mistake on my tax returns. I've made amends.' We certainly couldn't allow [that] to happen."

The statement of evidence was ready. The letter of resignation was ready. A 2:00 p.m. court date was set. But not a single soul in the country, except for the people directly involved, knew what was supposed to happen in that courtroom.

The media knew there was an Agnew-related hearing that afternoon, but they actually thought it was about them—specifically, a hearing for news organizations to argue why the judge should quash the subpoenas Agnew's lawyers had sent to reporters. The press showed up ready to cover that hearing, and the lawyers for the news organizations showed up at the counsel's table ready to plead their case.

And then, suddenly, at a little before two o'clock that afternoon, the vice president's attorneys walked into the courtroom.

The lawyers for the press "see us walking in," Marty London says, "and we sit at the near table, and they look at us with hostility! I mean, sneering, like *Grrrrr!* Just angry! And then, two federal marshals come over to them and they say, 'Pick up all your papers and move to the gallery,' and they're resistant, but these are federal marshals and the marshals do not explain why. They just said, 'Clear this table and clear it now! You can go stand in the back.'"

Once the media lawyers moved to the gallery, a surprising new team entered the courtroom: Attorney General Elliot Richardson, Assistant Attorney General Henry

Petersen, U.S. Attorney George Beall of Maryland, and Beall's three Assistant U.S. Attorneys, Barney Skolnik, Tim Baker, and Ron Liebman.

The prosecution took their seats at the table. The vice president's defense team was at their own table. The appointed time had arrived.

There was just one problem. "It's now two o'clock and I am sweating," Marty London says, "because at our table is me and Jay Topkis, and Jud Best is back in the clerk's office on the telephone. And it's two o'clock and somebody from this play is missing!"

The sequence of events had been painstakingly choreographed, each moment scripted and ordered to precision. Jud Best was posted in the clerk's office just off the courtroom because he was waiting to give the order over the phone to deliver Agnew's resignation letter to Secretary of State Henry Kissinger at the exact moment the vice president walked into the courtroom.

But the vice president . . . was nowhere to be found.

Ron Liebman and his colleagues had feared that something like this might happen. What if "he gets into court and he says, 'Well, wait a minute, I changed my mind. These are bogus charges. I don't know why I'm here. I'm the vice president of the United States. I'm immune from prosecution. Marshal, could you unlock that door please?'" Liebman was beginning to stew on this possibility, growing tense. "You know, we're dealing with the vice president of the United States. We are being as careful as we can be. We're on tenterhooks, right? We want this done just so. It had to be done just so or it wouldn't happen."

Agnew's own lawyers weren't sure what was up. "I was anxious," Marty London recalls. "I wouldn't say nervous, but I was anxious! . . . I can understand him not wanting to come into that courtroom. And I do get it, him not wanting to come into that courtroom and sit there at that table for fifteen minutes with all of those people staring at the back of his neck."

So everybody sat, for what seemed like an eternity but was in fact a bit more than a minute. At "2:01 exactly, in walks our client," London says. "And the people in the room, they gasped. It then became clear what this was about."

"There was a noticeable hush," Liebman recalls. "It was a surprise to so many people." As Spiro Agnew walked into the well of the courtroom, his resignation letter was officially given to Secretary of State Henry Kissinger. And then the historic proceedings began in the Baltimore courtroom.

George Beall submitted to the judge a copy of the official criminal complaint against Agnew, charging the vice president with one count of income tax evasion for the year 1967, the year before he was elected vice president.

The judge asked how Agnew wished to plead, and his defense lawyer, Jay Topkis, responded, "On behalf of the defendant, Your Honor, we lodge a plea of nolo contendere."

Judge Walter Hoffman asked whether the defendant understood that such a plea was "the full equivalent to a plea of guilty." Agnew himself responded, "I do, Your

Honor." Hoffman then led Agnew through a litany of questions clarifying the charge to which he was pleading and its consequences.

"You fully understand the plea of no contest?"

"I do, Your Honor."

"Do you fully understand the charge?"

"I do, Your Honor."

Satisfied by his responses, Judge Hoffman accepted Agnew's plea. And then what happened next was an almost-unheard-of event in federal court. The attorney general of the United States rose to act as lead prosecutor. "I am, like every other participant in these proceedings, deeply conscious of the critical national interests which surround them," Elliot Richardson began. He then submitted to the court the statement the Baltimore prosecutors had spent all night compiling and attempted to explain why the clear evidence of bribery contained within it was not being charged.

"In light of the serious wrongdoing shown by its evidence," Richardson said, "the government might have insisted, if permitted by the Court to do so, on pressing forward with the return of an indictment charging bribery and extortion. To have done this, however, would have likely inflicted upon the Nation serious and permanent scars. . . . It is unthinkable that this Nation should have been required to endure the anguish and uncertainty of a prolonged period in which the man next in line of succession to the presidency was fighting the charges brought against him by his own government.

"On the basis of these considerations," Richardson continued, "I am satisfied that the public interest is better served by this Court's acceptance of the defendant's plea of nolo contendere to a single-count information charging income tax evasion."

As to the requested sentence, Richardson bit the bullet, as he said he would. "I am firmly convinced that, under all the circumstances, leniency is justified." Agnew had taken the historic step of resignation, he said, and "to propose that a man who has suffered these penalties should, in addition, be incarcerated in a penal institution, however brief, is more than I, as head of the government's prosecution arm, can recommend or wish."

When Richardson was finished, Agnew himself rose to deliver a final statement.

"My decision to resign and enter a plea of nolo contendere rests on my firm belief that the public interest requires a swift disposition of the problems which are facing me," Agnew said. "I am advised that a full legal defense of the probable charges against me could consume several years. I am concerned that intense media interest in the case would distract public attention from important national problems to the country's detriment."

Agnew denied that he had ever extorted anyone or solicited any bribes, and said that he was accepting a plea deal because fighting the charges at trial "would seriously prejudice the national interest."

After Agnew had had his say, Judge Walter Hoffman turned to address the packed courtroom. While "some persons will criticize the result and the sentence to be imposed," Hoffman said, "it would be impossible to satisfy everyone."

In normal cases of lawyers—like Agnew—committing tax evasion, the judge said, his typical sentence would include a monetary fine, as well as a sentence of confinement. But, he continued, "I am persuaded that the national interests in the present case are so great and so compelling . . . that the ends of justice would be better served by making an exception to the general rule."

With that, Judge Hoffman instructed Spiro Agnew to stand and receive his sentence: a $10,000 fine and three years of unsupervised probation.

For the first time in American history, a sitting vice president appeared in federal court to answer criminal charges. For the first time, a vice president pleaded to a felony. And for the first time, a vice president resigned his office in disgrace. Agnew had arrived at the courthouse second in line to the presidency; he left several minutes later a private citizen and a convicted felon.

"It was a stunning, stunning development," says Agnew's lawyer Marty London.

Agnew trailed his attorneys out of the courthouse and made a brief statement to the reporters who gathered outside. "I categorically and flatly deny the assertions that have been made by the prosecutors," he said. "I will have nothing more to say at this point, I will make an address to the nation within a few days."

Agnew's own staff was just as surprised as the rest of the country, but a lot less forgiving. When he learned from another senior staffer that Agnew was on his way to Baltimore to plead and resign, David Keene pounded his fist on a desk: "Can't the son of a bitch have the balls to come tell us himself!"

Neither were members of Congress alerted in advance; the last they had heard from Agnew he wanted to be impeached. "There was disbelief on Capitol Hill," NBC News reported, "where most House and Senate members had come to believe the Vice President's assertions that he fully intended to fight the charges all the way."

"It was totally unexpected," the Democratic Senate majority leader, Mike Mansfield, said, "and I, uh, boy, I don't know what to say."

"We have a period of time when there is political erosion. Confidence and faith in the whole system has been challenged by many people," said the Republican senator Mark Hatfield, "and now, to have this kind of confirmation of the worst suspicions that some people have held is really a very profound impact on the whole country."

The reaction across the country reached across the spectrum. Stunned confusion from those just learning the news; elation from those who felt justice had finally been served; and absolute outrage from many of Agnew's supporters, who had stood behind him until the very end. *Agnew for president!*

"I'm just sick about it," one woman told a reporter. "I think he's a man of his word and I think they've all been doing the same thing ever since I started voting! And I think it's just too bad, I think he's a great man."

"I'm just, ohhhh, I'm just sick! I'm very unhappy," said

another woman. "I don't think it was necessary, I think it's a lot of political hogwash!"

The majority of the Republican Party, including many in Congress, was still standing with Agnew. He was, after all, the victim of a scurrilous witch hunt. And even though he had just pleaded no contest to a felony in open court, his supporters had been told to believe in his innocence no matter what facts were reported and to resent everything about this unfair prosecution. That sentiment didn't wear off even after Agnew himself had given up the game.

"The man seems to be railroaded or something," said one faithful supporter. "I don't know if this is all fact. A lot of insinuation is being brought out."

Whether they agreed with the outcome or not, there was one fact that remained indisputable. Spiro T. Agnew's short and spectacular political career was over.

It's probably not too dramatic to say it was over just in the nick of time, too. If you doubt that, consider this scene from the evening of October 20, 1973, just ten days after Agnew's resignation: J. T. Smith, Attorney General Elliot Richardson's top aide, secretly hurrying out of Justice Department headquarters with a stack of files stuffed under his arms. "I took my notes, put them in my briefcase, and walked out without being searched," Smith says. "I was sufficiently paranoid about the direction of the country I hid them in the attic of my house."

Earlier that same evening, President Nixon—in a fit of rage—had decided to throw a big monkey wrench into the Department of Justice in general and its investigation of

Watergate in particular. Nixon was furious that Special Prosecutor Archibald Cox was refusing to comply with the terms of a new agreement between the president and the Senate Watergate Committee. A summary of the White House tapes might be good enough for the Senate, Cox had said, but it was not good enough for the special prosecutor's office. He still wanted those tapes, and he was going to keep fighting all the way to the Supreme Court to get them. So Nixon fired Cox on the evening of October 20, 1973. Or actually, he called Attorney General Elliot Richardson and ordered him to fire Cox. Richardson refused, and when President Nixon pressed, he resigned in protest. His deputy attorney general, William Ruckelshaus, did the same.

The president was obliged to turn to the number three at the Department of Justice, the always-reliable solicitor general, Robert Bork, to follow through on Nixon's orders. Bork did. Archibald Cox was toast. Special agents from the FBI—acting on directions from the president— immediately sealed off Cox's offices, as well as those of Richardson and Ruckelshaus.

The country was suddenly, according to the NBC anchorman John Chancellor, in the midst of "the most serious constitutional crisis in its history." It was "a grave and profound crisis," Chancellor reported that evening on the *Nightly News*. "Nothing even remotely like it has happened in all of our history."

The Saturday Night Massacre, as the event came to be known, was a moment of high drama inside the Justice Department. That's what caused J. T. Smith to collect all of his papers before FBI agents could do it for him, and then spirit them out of the building to the safety of his home attic.

What's stunning to remember, what's almost never mentioned in the history books about that moment, is that when the Saturday Night Massacre happened, Elliot Richardson and his team had just secured the plea bargain and resignation of the sitting vice president . . . *ten days earlier.* There's no guarantee what would have happened if Nixon had torn up the Department of Justice a few weeks earlier, or if Agnew had strung out the negotiations with Richardson and his prosecutors a few weeks longer. There's no guarantee what would have happened if the attorney general had been somebody other than the ramrod-straight Elliot Richardson.

CHAPTER 15

★ ★ ★

WHY'D HE DO IT?

Here's a question worth considering: Why'd he do it? Not why did he extort and bribe and stay on the take even after he got to the White House. That's pretty obvious, given the kind of man Spiro Agnew was—tidily summed up by the assessment of one venerable and gimlet-eyed Maryland pol on the occasion of Agnew's death: "Lightning kept striking this guy who never had a machine, an organization or a record. He was a little hustler out of Baltimore County who made it to the White House, with no anchor, no mooring, no core. Gives politics a bad name."

The real question worth considering is this: Why did this hustler, this counterpunching political-pugilist tough guy, finally knuckle under and become the first vice president in history to resign in disgrace?

Agnew had his own explanation, which grew increasingly dramatic as the years went on. The story he told centered on the ten days or so after he returned from that rejuvenating trip to Southern California where he played golf with Sinatra and whipped the Republican women's convention into a proper lathered frenzy.

The federal bribery investigation was closing in on Agnew just then. The grand jury was about to reopen. The threat of indictment was hanging over his neck like a sharp scythe. Solicitor General Robert Bork was in the process of eviscerating his best legal argument—his immunity argument—in federal court. Oh, and Vice President Agnew was barely on speaking terms with the man to whom he owed his place in the White House. Richard Nixon had long since ceased supporting his vice president in public; in private, the president had made it abundantly and increasingly clear that he wanted Agnew to resign.

The way Agnew later told the story, the morning of October 4, 1973, was the turning point for him. That was the day, Agnew later explained, that the White House chief of staff, Alexander Haig, delivered a message that "sent a chill through my body." Haig summoned a close adviser of Agnew's, Mike Dunn, to his West Wing office that day.

"The clock is running," Haig said, according to Dunn's memorialization of the meeting. The evidence the Justice Department now had "was massive"; prosecutors believed they had "an ironclad case for conviction." Once Agnew was indicted, Haig told Dunn, "it will be too late . . . to do this gracefully." The vice president needed to resign, or "we are off to the races and cannot control the situation any longer. Anything may be in the offing. It can, and will, get nasty and dirty. Don't think that the game cannot be played from here."

When Dunn briefed him after the meeting, Agnew later recalled, his aide said Haig "also reminded him" exactly who it was that Agnew was disobeying. "The president has a lot of power," Haig had said. "Don't forget that."

Agnew said later he took Haig's pointed reference to the president's "power" as a direct threat to his personal safety. "I feared for my life," he wrote in his memoirs. "If a decision had been made to eliminate me—through an automobile accident, a fake suicide, or whatever—the order would not have been traced back to the White House any more than the 'get Castro' orders were ever traced to their source." He was "close enough" to the presidency to know that a chief executive "could order the CIA to carry out missions that were very unhealthy for people who were considered enemies."

In so many words, Agnew was alleging that he only resigned the vice presidency to save his own life—because Richard Nixon had threatened to have him *assassinated* if he didn't resign. Seriously? "I didn't know what General

Haig meant when he said 'anything may be offing, things may get nasty and dirty,'" Agnew said in a television interview in 1980, years after his resignation. "There's no doubt in my mind that these things are possible. I don't say it was a probability, but I do say it was a possibility."

Asked if he thought "there were men around Richard Nixon—either in the White House staff or in the official mechanism of the CIA—who were capable of killing a vice president of the United States if they felt he was an embarrassment," Agnew answered somberly, "I don't doubt that at all."

Agnew said that he was so fearful at the time that he bought a gun for protection. "I've never carried the handgun," he admitted. "I thought it was sufficient that people would know I had the permit to carry one."

"I've never said it was a *probability* that my life was in danger," he hedged in another interview. "I said it was one of the factors that crossed my mind and it was the straw that broke the camel's back after all the pressures that had been put on me."

And so, the ridiculous supposed Oval Office murder plot became the story Spiro Agnew would promote about his resignation, in multiple national television appearances, long after he was otherwise gone from public life. It wasn't enough that he couldn't admit that his own actions, his own crimes, had brought historic disrepute on the institution he served. He had to go further than that, to try to make himself seem like just another one of Richard Nixon's innocent victims.

For his part, Al Haig told a reporter for *The Washington Post* that Agnew's claim "was the most preposterous thing he had ever heard of."

Agnew's aide Mike Dunn—who in Agnew's telling had received and passed on the supposed murder threat—agreed with Haig that the whole thing was laughable. "In my mind, there was never any threat of bodily harm. The idea never entered my consciousness," he told the same reporter. "In all fairness," he said, "the man was distraught at the time, as he had every reason to be." But even years later, this was the story Spiro Agnew wanted to tell: Richard Nixon's inner circle pressured him to resign, and when he refused to do it, they threatened his life. Sure thing, Ted, whatever you say.

There is, however, a competing explanation for why Spiro Agnew called it quits when he did, declining to even try to fight the charges against him. And the alternate explanation does involve a perceived threat to Agnew from a three-letter federal agency, but not the CIA.

Throughout the time that Agnew was under scrutiny from U.S. Attorney George Beall and his team of young federal prosecutors, a separate Agnew investigation was happening parallel to that federal criminal probe. Special agents from the Internal Revenue Service had been quietly and diligently combing through Agnew's past, hoping to find the answer to one burning question: How exactly had the vice president been spending all of his ill-gotten gains? These were the same IRS agents who had turned up the first smoking-gun evidence of the bribery scheme against Agnew's successor, Dale Anderson, back in Baltimore

County. These were the same agents whose digging led the U.S. Attorney's office to Lester Matz and Jerry Wolff and, eventually, Spiro Agnew. They knew Agnew's cash was coming in as bribes, but they were also looking into how he was spending that bribery money and the potentially crucial question of whether he was evading taxes in the process. Financial records in hand, the agents fanned out across the country to find receipts. "They were looking at every Coca-Cola that he had purchased," Marty London recalls.

"By nature, it's a very slow, laborious process," says Ron Liebman of this kind of "net worth" investigation. The agents slowly documented "where every penny came in and where every penny came out." Eventually, unsurprisingly, they hit a nerve.

The IRS investigators found what looked to be evidence of a secret life. Nothing fancy. Just the same sort of banal antics that defined the Mid-century Modern Madman: mistresses, sports cars, expensive gifts. "There was jewelry, too," says Tim Baker. "A woman's watch which [Agnew's wife] Judy never got."

This wasn't a trail of evidence the Baltimore prosecutors were eager to pursue. "These guys, they have all these personal peccadilloes, you know, they have money and power and they do stupid things," says Liebman. "And we came across financial evidence of that and we heard some stories. One of them quite bizarre." He won't elaborate, but it was the sort of behavior that "involves sex. It involves mistresses. It involves all kinds of bad behavior.

"We investigated it. We confirmed it as much as we

could. But we never decided to use it." There was never even a real debate—which, Liebman knows, might seem odd today. "Pre–Monica Lewinsky—unlike Ken Starr, I guess—we just said, 'This is not a part of the case.'"

Agnew and his attorneys, meanwhile, were very much aware that the tax men had been rummaging around in his personal life. "I knew that there was an IRS net worth investigation; obviously the vice president knew that as well," Marty London says. "That's the thing you're trying to shed. That's what anyone who is in that tax bind wants to get rid of."

Agnew was so concerned that he went to Nixon to address this aspect of the investigation. He complained directly to the president, in private, that the prosecutors were tracking down everything he ever bought and every detail of his personal life. "Was Agnew worried that that might all come out? Probably he was," Liebman says. "Maybe he was worried that we would make it public."

"He wanted to get on with his life; he wanted to get the hounds off his back," says London. "He wanted the end of the IRS investigation." And so maybe that's what collapsed his defenses and made him decide to quit. Sounds cooler, though, if it was because Nixon was going to send the CIA to fake-suicide him. That would at least sell more books?

CHAPTER 16

★ ★ ★

DISAPPEARING ACT

W hat we are about to see has never before happened in American history," explained the *NBC News* anchor John Chancellor on the evening of October 15, 1973, as he prepared the country for one more surreal moment in what had already been a year that beggared belief.

Congress and the executive branch had been skirmishing most of the year, in the courts and on television, over an endless parade of scandal. Each day seemed to test our constitutional system in some entirely novel fashion. Five days earlier, for instance, for the first time in American history, a vice president had been ushered out of his office by way of a federal courtroom.

And now Chancellor was preparing the audience for another unprecedented happening: a live address from that former vice president, and current convicted felon. Spiro Agnew, as a private citizen, could no longer expect the networks to necessarily heed his request for airtime, and he certainly wasn't going to be speaking to the nation from his old office in the White House. There really was no protocol in place for how a disgraced former vice president might go about engineering this speech. So Agnew simply asked for the airtime from his old nemeses at the three major networks, and—given the inescapable historical import of the moment—they granted it.

Agnew made the short drive to the NBC News bureau in suburban Washington, D.C., sat down in front of a generic blue TV studio curtain, and explained himself to the nation. "I do not want to spend these last moments with you in a paroxysm of bitterness," he began. Then came the "but." "But I do think there are matters related to my resignation that are misunderstood. It is important to me and, I believe, to the country that these misconceptions be corrected."

The former vice president did not express remorse that night, or acknowledge that he had perhaps acted improperly at times. He passed on his opportunity to invite calm or unity. Made no effort to tamp the fresh hot rage of his supporters. That wouldn't be Spiro Agnew. Instead, he took this opposite of a victory lap as one more opportunity to stoke resentment.

"Late this summer," Agnew intoned, "my fitness to continue in office came under attack when accusations against me made in the course of a grand jury investigation were improperly and unconscionably leaked in detail to the news media." With his voice rising, he continued, "The news media editorially deplored these violations of the traditional secrecy of such investigations, but at the same time many of the most prestigious of them were ignoring their own counsel by publishing every leak they could get their hands on."

Spiro Agnew left public life the same way he entered it; his gut instincts and a self-described "subliminal type of intelligence" drove him to deny any accusations against him, no matter their actual truth, and then to attack, by name, and often in personal terms, his antagonists. The counterpuncher flailing away at enemies real and invented.

No matter that he had acknowledged just days earlier in open court that his plea of nolo contendere was "the full equivalent to a plea of guilty." Agnew conceded no such thing in his televised address. He was "fully aware" of the meaning of his plea, he explained, but had chosen it solely "for the purpose of that negotiated proceeding in Baltimore; it does not represent a confession of any guilt whatever for any other purpose. I made the plea because it was the only way to quickly resolve the situation."

The whole experience was a "nightmare come true," Agnew said, and he wanted to make sure it never happened to any future occupant of the White House. He suggested, in closing, that future prosecutors be "restricted" from targeting other politicians the way he had just been brought down. It would be decades before any other White House denizen would suggest that presidents and vice presidents should be immune not only from federal prosecution but also from federal investigation.

After his speech that night, Agnew supporters told reporters they were still behind the vice president turned convict, 100 percent. A salesman from Forest Hill, Maryland, answered a *New York Times* reporter's query about the speech by turning it back around on his questioner: "Part of the trouble is *you* people."

AFTER THE RESIGNATION and then the queasy-making TV speech, the former vice president remained in the nation's capital, for months, as a "quasi" public official. He was gifted a small government staff, round-the-clock Secret Service protection, and a taxpayer-funded office just a block from the White House. All the result of a gentleman's agreement he had brokered with Richard Nixon.

The Secret Service detail was assigned for an "undetermined" period, and the office and staff, Agnew later wrote, were necessary "so that my vice-presidential papers could be catalogued and the business of winding up my nearly five years in the second-highest office could be done in an orderly fashion."

The end of 1973 was a time when there were plenty of avant-garde oddities in the nation's capital. President Nix-

THE WHITE HOUSE

WASHINGTON

Octh 10, 1973

Dear Ted —

On such a sad occasion our hearts go out to you and your splendid family — Take comfort from the fact that your dedicated service as Vice President will in the end be more remembered than those unfortunate events which currently dominate the news. In these next few months and the years ahead you will find out who your real friends are. Count me and the entire Nixon family among them. You have been wounded but I predict you will recover and fight again another day — RN

Nixon's farewell letter to his criminally convicted vice president. It reads, in full, "Dear Ted: On such a sad occasion our hearts go out to you and your splendid family. Take comfort from the fact that your dedicated service as Vice President will in the end be more remembered than those unfortunate events which currently dominate the news. In these next few months and the years ahead you will find out who your real friends are. Count me and the entire Nixon family among them. You have been wounded but I predict you will recover and fight again another day." —RN on's frantic efforts to wriggle free from impeachment and possible criminal indictment were the most visible, of course. But the sight of Spiro Agnew still traipsing around Washington with an official limousine, government-issue staff, and a Secret Service code name struck many as a particularly bizarre ring of this dystopian political circus.

"He still comes downtown almost daily to an office," *The Baltimore Sun* reported in early November, weeks after Agnew's assumed exit from public life. "[He] occasionally slips out to play tennis at a Washington hotel. The phone often goes unanswered in the middle of the day."

Agnew wasn't at all interested in shedding the trappings of high office, no matter how many eyebrows he raised or how many people he enraged. When he visited his devoted pal Frank Sinatra in Chicago "with two carloads of Secret Service agents," Agnew didn't even bother to explain. "I'm here to relax and have a good time," he told incredulous reporters. A columnist for the *Chicago Sun-Times* wrote, "It probably is the first time the Secret Service has guarded a felon without first snapping on handcuffs."

"How long the agents will be with Agnew isn't known," griped one Indiana newspaper editorial. "What irks, however, is that the kind of protection he seems to need from the agents could just as easily—easier, in fact—been provided in prison."

Neither was Agnew in any particular rush to get his affairs in order. The task of going through old papers and records was made slightly more difficult by the fact that the pile was still growing. Letters from sympathetic supporters continued to arrive daily and had to be added to the file. As did Agnew's letters of response, which he seemed eager to offer into the public record. "Your support and encouragement meant a great deal to me," he wrote to one correspondent. "I can only reaffirm my innocence to you and hope, in this complex and confusing situation, that you will try to understand that I believe the actions I have taken are in the best interest of the Nation."

"It is difficult for me; but I must accept the inevitable, rational conclusion that our system of justice does not always guarantee a fair result," he replied to another, at peak sanctimony. "In my case, the malicious leaks to the media, the blatant enticements of immunity for those inextricably caught, the political expedience which led the Congress to refuse me an objective hearing, all prohibited the traditional safeguard of a presumption of innocence. Perhaps someday I will be in a position to explain more fully the unusual confluence of events which caused me to take the course I did." (This was before he decided to start telling people that Nixon was plotting to kill him.)

Although Agnew was certainly enjoying his unusual convicted/emeritus vice presidential privileges and trappings, cold reality finally came crashing down during a trip to Palm Springs in February 1974.

The former vice president was reportedly making a quick jaunt to celebrate the eightieth birthday of the comedian Jack Benny at a party thrown at Frank Sinatra's desert estate. But word got out that he had decided to make the trip west an eight-day vacation and a chance to get some quiet time to work on the new suspense novel he was shopping to publishers. When Agnew arrived in California with his regular coterie of Secret Service along for the ride—as many as twenty-one agents, by one count—things began to go sideways on him. Especially after the Government Accounting Office reported that the cost of protecting the disgraced vice president was running about $45,000 a month.

Democratic members of Congress decided they'd had enough. "This is an outrageous act," Representative John Moss protested on the floor of the House. He called the Palm Springs trip, and Agnew's continued Secret Service protection, "an affront to every taxpaying American." Headlines out of Southern California piled up until Secretary of the Treasury George Shultz, acting at the direction of the Nixon White House, hastily announced that Agnew's most egregious perk was officially being pulled.

"Suddenly one evening," Agnew later recalled, "the Secret Service with me received orders to cease my protection at midnight. The White House communications people came in that same evening and pulled out the White House phones, and the agents left at midnight. I had not been notified by anyone until the head of my detail informed me."

Spiro Agnew was now finally on his own. The sudden expiration of his free government entourage apparently acted as a slap-in-the-face reminder of some other central facts of his life: he was unemployed, stripped of his law license in Maryland, and nowhere near paid up on his legal bills.

"I needed one thing urgently," he later said, "a way to make a living."

The first financial lifeline tossed to Agnew came by way of the fifth (and perhaps the favorite) husband of one of the Hollywood-famous Gabor sisters. Sister Eva, an actress and socialite famous for her recent star turn on TV's *Green Acres,* had just married an international businessman named Frank Jameson who, on the honeymoon, happened to read about Agnew's money woes. So the couple swung through Washington on the way home, and—seemingly on a whim—Jameson offered Agnew a job. "I told him I was getting involved in international trade," Jameson said, "and he said that sounded like something he would be interested in."

Asked if he was concerned about hiring one of the country's most conspicuous felons, Jameson said, "There's no pancake so thin that it doesn't have two sides." Jameson was a bit unsure about exactly what the former vice president would do on the job, but he thought Agnew's "talent to communicate with people" could be put to good use. Agnew's record proved of greater concern, however, to the board members of Jameson's new company, who not so subtly suggested that Agnew wasn't a good fit. "I resigned to save [Jameson] from embarrassment," Agnew explained. So Agnew lost that job. Goodbye, City Life. But he had a new grudge to nurse. "This sort of extra punishment was so unfair, it made me furious," he wrote. "They had knocked me down; now they wanted to kick me."

The question of where Agnew would pop up next became the source of mild, or perhaps morbid, intrigue. Not just in the general public, but inside the federal government as well.

The Department of State received a cable from a somewhat bemused official at the U.S. embassy in the Venezuelan capital of Caracas a month after Agnew's final ousting. The former vice president had surfaced in the city, apparently in pursuit of a *movie* project with Sinatra. According to local reports, the embassy informed the State Department, Agnew was preparing to star in a Hollywood film called *The Caracas Connection*. The novice actor would play the part of a "seemingly respectable citizen later revealed to be head of a narcotics ring." The ambassador cautioned that he wasn't able to personally confirm that Agnew was, in fact, set to make his on-screen debut. But apparently he figured it was worth keeping tabs on it at Foggy Bottom, just in case. In the end, no such movie was ever produced.

There was then a brief flurry of speculation that Agnew might be moving from politics to sports—specifically, to the upstart World Football League, which was being launched to compete with the NFL. Agnew and Sinatra reportedly discussed the prospect of partnering to own a franchise based in Los Angeles. As with the movie, though, the gridiron venture was little more than a rumor. It, too, came to naught.

Really needing to make some money, Agnew did actually try his hand as a novelist. His political thriller, *The Canfield Decision*, centered on a fictional vice president who—and this was not much of a stretch—was eventually crippled by his own ambition. The protagonist, Porter Canfield ("wealthy, handsome and self-assured"), did manage to bed the "beautiful, amber-eyed" secretary of health, education, and welfare. Agnew was sarcastically credited for "extreme inventiveness," in a *New York Times* review, but that was as good as it got. The book was widely panned as a "mean-spirited piece of work" in which Agnew bitterly took aim at some of his favorite old targets. "The book is anti-press, anti-Semitic, anti-woman and anti-black," wrote one reviewer.

Apparently unmoved by *The Canfield Decision*'s lack of critical or commercial success, Agnew signed on to write a second book. This would be not another novel but instead a memoir. He titled it *Go Quietly . . . or Else* (it was dedicated not to his wife or family but "to Frank Sinatra"). The Agnew memoir, published in 1980, recounted and revived his battles with the "enemies" who brought about his demise—including the allegedly murderous Richard Nixon.

The blowback from *Go Quietly . . . or Else* was considerably more damaging to Agnew than was the blowback from *The Canfield Decision,* and not only because the plot of his memoir was even more ridiculous than the one in the novel. The real problem for Agnew with *Go Quietly* was that the author made a few critical mistakes concerning an old attorney-friend of his named George White. *Go Quietly* was so mean-spirited about his old pal that White filed a $17.5 million libel suit against Agnew and his publisher. White charged defamation of character, invasion of privacy, and injurious falsehood. The book was rife with "false statements and distortions from cover to cover," he alleged.

Agnew never had to pay up, but that was only because

his old friend agreed to accept a public letter of apology as settlement. "I hope you will accept this letter as a statement of regret on my part for any misunderstanding that may have arisen," Agnew wrote. "I also realize that I should have checked beyond my own recollections to verify the facts."

But there was one other mistake Spiro Agnew made in his memoir as regards George White. White had been one of Agnew's attorneys during the scandal that led to his resignation. In the memoir, Agnew wrote a detailed scene about the moment when White first alerted him to his coming problems, way back in February 1973, when the investigation in Baltimore County was just getting started. This was before Agnew was implicated in any criminality, but there was already concern that Lester Matz and Jerry Wolff might tell what they knew. George White, in his capacity as Agnew's personal attorney, thought he should get Agnew's side of the story.

"White interrogated me closely," Agnew wrote in his memoir. "'This is very serious,' he said. 'I want you to level with me about it.'

"'George, I am leveling with you about it,' I said, becoming indignant. 'There is nothing to this. They are apparently in trouble, and they are trying to put the heat on me to extricate them, but I can't do anything for them.'"

No doubt Agnew felt it helped his cause to get that little bit of fiction out there again in 1980. But he had made a critical error at a critical time. By writing about the conversation with White, Agnew had waived any attorney-client privilege that protected exchanges with his lawyer. And that mistake was a very big reason why Spiro Agnew, finally, would get some measure of comeuppance.

Before that point, Agnew of course had lost his job and the good parts of his reputation, but he also avoided any serious financial penalty for his considerable financial crimes. When he walked away from that federal courtroom on October 10, 1973, not only did he have his liberty, but his only financial penalty was a $10,000 fine, a slap on the wrist.

That was something one young attorney was unable to let slide. For years. He just couldn't let it go; he couldn't abide it.

John Banzhaf happened to be in the gallery of the Baltimore courthouse that fateful autumn day back in 1973, when Agnew pleaded *nolo* and resigned. Banzhaf was a law professor in his early thirties then, teaching a course on "legal activism" at George Washington University. His course was a primer for students on how to shepherd legal actions through the courts in order to effect change on issues of public interest. Banzhaf's own legal activism was not merely academic. He had led the successful effort, a few years earlier, to get tobacco ads banned from television. Professor Banzhaf was at the Baltimore court on October 10 when Agnew made his surprise appearance because he had already filed several motions related to the Agnew case. He had first filed a motion calling for a special prosecutor to replace Elliot Richardson (who, Banzhaf believed, had a conflict of interest), and he had just filed another motion to quash the subpoenas that Agnew's lawyers had sent to news reporters. He drove to Baltimore that day for a hearing on the subpoena issue.

"I showed up and initially they would not let me in," Banzhaf says. After insisting on his *bona fides,* "I was reluctantly let into the courtroom, but with a very solemn warning that if I attempted to say anything, if I stood up, if I did anything at all, there were two big marshals behind me and they would immediately take me out of the courtroom." He had never encountered such resistance. "I was told in very strong language, 'Don't stand. Don't say anything. Don't try to have any role.'"

At just after two o'clock that afternoon, when Vice President Spiro Agnew entered the courtroom, Banzhaf says he realized the actual purpose of the day's proceedings and—not incidentally for him—that the motions he had filed in the Agnew case were "clearly moot." So he sat quietly in the gallery and watched history being made. A sitting vice president resigned his office and pleaded to a felony. He was sentenced on the spot, in what had obviously been worked out between Agnew and the prosecutors: three years of unsupervised probation and a $10,000 fine. It all happened so fast it made Banzhaf's head spin. But as time went on, questions continued to nag at him. Agnew was not going to be sent to jail for his crimes or assigned a major fine. He wasn't even going to be asked to pay back the money he had taken in bribes?

What was the punishment here? Resigning from office? But was that it? And was that fair?

Banzhaf put these questions to his students at George

Washington University's law school, and they were as perplexed as he was. "They said to me, 'Professor Banzhaf, if somebody robs a bank and he's given a plea deal, he's at least required to give back the money!' Agnew was governor and vice president. Shouldn't he be held to an even higher standard? They were outraged that he was allowed to get off on a minor plea, no time, and keep all the ill-gotten gains!"

Under Banzhaf's supervision, a handful of law students at George Washington University decided they were going to make a project out of Spiro Agnew. Banzhaf's class devised a plan to sue Agnew in state court, to force him to pay back the bribe money he had taken while he was a public servant. Their first move was to lobby Maryland's governor, Marvin Mandel, to bring the lawsuit: After all, when Agnew was shaking down those Baltimore County contractors, it was the state that was being defrauded of honest services. The taxpayers of Maryland should get that money back.

Governor Mandel heard the students out. And then told them no, his administration was not interested in pushing the case. "We were literally bewildered," Banzhaf says. "I recall riding back in the car and the students are saying, 'Well, why didn't they bring it? We don't understand. What's going on?' And I'm their professor who's supposed to know these things, and of course I had no answer for them. I could not figure out why they wouldn't want to bring the action."

The answer became obvious only a few years later, when Governor Mandel himself was found to have committed a very Agnew-esque criminal breach of the public trust to help some buddies who wanted to build a racetrack. He was indicted by the same Baltimore prosecutors who took down Agnew. Like Agnew, Mandel was removed from office, but unlike his gubernatorial predecessor Mandel wasn't so lucky as to avoid a prison sentence: he served nearly two years in federal custody.

But the Mandel misfire did not faze John Banzhaf or his now-galvanized student activists. "I said, 'Well, don't give up. Go back in that law library and see if there's some way we can still get Agnew to pay up.'" His students emerged from the stacks with a centuries-old British legal principle in hand. The principle "literally dates back to the Crusades," Banzhaf says, and it allows some other interested party to take up the cause of a wronged entity if that entity "was unwilling or unable to do it." According to this precedent, Banzhaf and his students believed they could bring an action "on behalf of the Maryland taxpayers" even if Maryland wouldn't consent to it. The taxpayers themselves had standing. The State of Maryland might not be willing to go after Spiro Agnew on behalf of its own citizens, but these students would do it *for* them. In 1976, the law students filed suit against Spiro Agnew in the name of several Maryland taxpayers. This was "a chance for the little guys to get back at the big guys," one volunteer plaintiff explained.

It took years for the case to wind its way through the courts, but in April 1981, seven and a half years after Agnew's resignation, a judge ruled that Agnew had, in fact, defrauded the people of Maryland. He ordered Agnew to pay back everything he had taken as governor and vice president. Agnew briefly protested the ruling, but ended up writing a check to the state for $268,482. (The bribe money plus interest.)

"I certainly realized that it was an uphill battle that many might regard as fruitless if not frivolous," Banzhaf says of the suit. But he had won cases people saw as fruitless or frivolous before. "It was at least worth a try." Banzhaf and his students deserve credit for getting that money back for the citizens of Maryland. But the young attorneys and attorneys-to-be got an extra little cherry on top for the rest of the country.

They got what amounted to a confession.

Not from Agnew, of course, who refused to testify. They got it by calling George White, Agnew's former lawyer, who was no longer shielded from telling what he knew by attorney-client privilege because of his star turn in Agnew's *Go Quietly . . . or Else* memoir.

In court, White testified to what Spiro Agnew had really said when White first told him that the kickback scheme was about to be revealed. White's version tracked with Agnew's to a point. And then it diverged. White testified that he had in fact confronted the vice president by saying, "Ted, this is terribly serious, you've got to level with me, I've got to know the truth," just as Agnew wrote in his memoir. But while Agnew had written that his response was to deny having solicited bribes or taken kickbacks, George White said Agnew gave a much different answer. According to White, Agnew had actually said to him, "It's been going on for a thousand years. What they told you is true."

There it was, at last, nearly a decade after his resignation. After all the angry denials and counterpunching and demonizing the Justice Department and the press that reported on his case. After all the claims that he, Spiro Agnew, was the real victim here, there was his admission of guilt.

Reporters chased George White outside the courtroom that day to ask him if what he had just said on the witness stand was really true. White said it was. But why should we believe you? the reporters wanted to know. Because, White said, speeding away, "I was under oath."

LEGACIES

In a few short months in the summer and fall of 1973, Spiro Agnew rewrote the rules for how a White House occupant can respond, and fight back, when his own Justice Department comes knocking. Damn the investigators. Damn the press. Damn the opposition. Damn the facts. Hang in there, baby! A legitimate investigation, it turns out, can be smeared and muddied up with a simple but aggressive counteroffensive—one that privileges feelings over facts, base loyalty over evidence, and obstruction over cooperation.

Agnew went beyond denying the "damned lies" about his criminal activity; he also rallied his supporters against the public officials in the Justice Department who were working on his case. He raised the specter of politically motivated "leaks" from bad actors on the inside. He attacked witnesses said to be cooperating with the government as "crazy" and self-motivated while also claiming he barely even knew them. He demanded that the investigators be investigated and purged from the government pay-roll if need be. He demeaned the professional and personal integrity of specific officials in the chain of command on his prosecution. Their allegedly dodgy behavior, Agnew insisted, should cast doubt on all of the allegations against him.

The assault on his own government was paired with ceaseless attacks on the media, stoking his supporters' distrust of legitimate reporting. He portrayed the press itself as one of his chief adversaries, encouraging crowds at his events to shows of open hostility toward journalists. He threatened reporters covering his case with subpoenas and even jail time.

And—not incidentally—he did all this at the time of the Watergate crisis. Spiro Agnew attempted to survive his own scandal by waging a concerted attack on the institutions of American life and government that were trying to hold the small-d democratic line and thereby hold the country together at that particularly tenuous time in our nation's history.

Ultimately, Agnew failed to save himself. But he left a scorched-earth battle plan for any corrupt officeholder that followed:

Attack the investigation as a witch hunt.

Obstruct it behind the scenes.

Attack individual investigators in personal terms.

Attack the credibility of the Justice Department itself.

Attack the media informing Americans about the case.

Punch back. Hard. Until either you are broken or the system is.

In the quarter century after his ignominious resignation from the vice presidency, Agnew continued to add ornament and object to his wider legacy. He didn't change the basic purport of that legacy much, though, because he remained true to his character right to the end. He chased money the rest of his life, and did so with little or no shame. His main source of income in the years after his resignation was a small company he started back in Maryland called Pathlite Inc. The sign on the door of his office read, REAL ESTATE, but the venture was actually a consulting firm, through which Agnew arranged financial marriages between wealthy American businessmen and wealthy foreign interests with whom he had brushed shoulders during his time in the White House.

Agnew flung himself all over the world, to Venezuela, Greece, the United Kingdom, and the Middle East, wherever he might snuffle up a lucrative deal to enrich himself and his politically connected clients. He did have some success as a roving international "middleman," but as in his ruined political career his business dealings generally had a strong whiff of turpitude.

Just for instance: In 1984, for a commission in the neighborhood of $800,000, Agnew helped outfit Saddam Hussein's Iraqi Army with military uniforms produced in Communist Romania. The 1984 deal involved a pair of former Nixon White House officials, including the former attorney general (and fellow ex-convict) John Mitchell, who had served a Watergate-related stint in federal prison.

The Saddam-Romania transaction was ultimately given a final push by Richard Nixon himself, who wrote personal letters of support for the deal to the ostentatiously corrupt and murderous Romanian dictator, Nicolae Ceauşescu. (Nixon later claimed he didn't know Agnew was involved in the transaction.)

Perhaps Agnew's most malodorous second act, though, took place elsewhere in the Middle East. In the late 1970s and early 1980s, the private citizen turned businessman Spiro Agnew wore a path between his home state of Maryland and the Kingdom of Saudi Arabia. As vice president, Agnew had forged ties with the Saudi royal family. As a disgraced former vice president, he used his newly formed "real estate" company to try to leverage those ties into personal profit. Pathlite CEO Agnew was a frequent sight in the Saudi capital in the decade after his resignation, pursing one business deal after another.

One of his campaigns in the kingdom proved particularly, nauseatingly awful, even by Agnew standards. It began in July 1980, when Agnew sent a short and urgent telegram from his Pathlite offices to Saudi Arabia's chief of royal protocol. "It would be deeply appreciated if Your Excellency could arrange for me to have an audience with his Royal Highness, Prince Fah'd, as soon as possible after the Eid holidays," Agnew wrote. "The matter to be discussed involves a personal emergency that is of critical importance to me. In the past, His Royal Highness has assured me that he would be available should I need to see him."

Agnew was a little short on cash, having recently paid back a $200,000 loan from Frank Sinatra. His career as an author was turning out to be a dud. The George Washington law students were busy in the Maryland courts trying to shake the change out of his pockets. And his old pal George White had filed his $17.5 million lawsuit a few weeks earlier.

The response was most welcome: "We can arrange for you to have an audience with His Royal Highness" the next month.

The reason he wanted to see the Saudi king was not for business per se, but Agnew did have an idea he hoped could be lucrative nonetheless and of value to the Saudi royal family. It was fueled by Agnew's two specialties: greed and slander. His pitch is spelled out in black and white in a letter Agnew drafted to the crown prince and then kept in his personal files, uncovered for the first time here. Spiro Agnew proposed to the Saudis that they support him in waging a spectacular propaganda campaign, back in the United States. The target? American Jews. He was just the man to do it.

His removal from office years earlier, Agnew claims in the letter, had been due not to his own misconduct but rather to "unremitting Zionist efforts to destroy me." America's Jews had orchestrated his removal because he was not pro-Israel enough, and Attorney General Elliot Richardson had gladly taken up their cause. "The Zionists in the United States," Agnew wrote to the Saudi royal, "had to get me out of there so I would not succeed Nixon. . . . I was framed and driven from office."

Agnew goes on to outline a Jewish conspiracy "to bleed me of my resources," so that he would be unable "to con-

August 25, 1980

His Royal Highness,
Prince Fahad bin Abdulaziz
Kingdom of Saudi Arabia

Your Highness:

Because of urgent problems at home, I regret
that I am unable to prolong my stay in Taif to meet
with Your Highness as planned. However, at the request
of Sheikh Ahmed Abdul Wahab, I am writing this letter
to explain the principal reasons for my urgent request
to see you. My necessary departure is, to a great extent, caused by the same difficulties that face me at
home.

Your Highness is already familiar with the unremitting Zionist efforts to destroy me. These well organized assaults began after my official visit to the
Kingdom in 1971, and they have accelerated since the
publication of my book, "Go Quietly, Or Else" this year.

During the time I was under attack from former
Attorney General Elliot Richardson in 1973, the reason
for their need to drive me out was stated by Richardson
several times. He said that I could not be trusted to
act properly in the middle east – meaning the October
war, which was raging at the time. Nixon was helpless
at the time because of his own Watergate problem, which
I was not involved in. Therefore, I was framed and driven from office. The reason was that the Zionists in the
United States knew that I would never agree to the con-
tinuance of the unfair and disastrous favoring of Israel,
and they had to get me out of there so that I would not
succeed Nixon – who they knew would be forced out also.

Since 1974, the Zionists have orchestrated a well-
organized attack on me – the idea being to use law suits
to bleed me of my resources to continue my effort to inform the American people of their control of the media
and other influential secotrs of American society. They
have filed four major law suits, one of which I have already
won after a four year battle and a cost of over $50 thou-
sand dollars in legal fees. Three remain open, the latest
being a 17 million dollar libel action filed by a lawyer
alleging that he was damaged by my book. I am sure that
this damage suit was encouraged by the Bnai Brith. The
net result of all these actions, and other complaints ar-
ising out of 1973, is that I have been financially disabled.
I do not have any resources left to continue the fight and
they are near to attaining their objective to silence me.

Draft of a letter that former vice president Spiro T. Agnew wrote to the
Saudi crown prince in August 1980

tinue my effort to inform the American people of their control of the media and other influential sectors of American society." Finally, he gets to the point: "I need desperately your financial support so that I can continue to fight."

Specifically, the former vice president writes, he needs $2 million in a secret Swiss bank account. He explains that funneling the funds through foreign banks will ensure that none of the money is traceable to the Saudi royal family. "If Your Highness is willing to help me but this method is not suitable," he adds, "I would be grateful for any idea that would give me about $200,000 a year for the next three years. I do so want to continue my fight against the Zionist enemies who are destroying my once great nation."

He concludes with a "congratulations to Your Highness on the clear and courageous call to Jihad"—a reference to the crown prince's call, days earlier, for an economic holy war against Israel.

So the answer to the question Whatever happened to old Spiro Agnew? is, at least in part, that he went on to market himself internationally as an influential American anti-Semite for hire. Nice. He would enlist the help of a foreign power to support his efforts to stir up hatred of Jews in America and profit handsomely in the venture. It also appears, from the subsequent correspondence in Agnew's files, that the Saudi government came through. At least a little bit.

Just a month after his first outreach, Agnew drafted a letter of thanks to the crown prince. "It is difficult for me to find the right words to adequately express my gratitude for the prompt response from Your Highness to my communication," he wrote. "I'm now in a position to meet my obligations for about six months under the framework set forth in my letter to you."

He added that he would try to drum up additional consulting business in the kingdom to give himself "the resources to continue the battle against the Zionist community here in the U.S." He received a final letter back from the Saudi crown prince warmly wishing him great "success" in his efforts.

This newfound evidence of Agnew's then-clandestine efforts is not just revealing of his basic nature; it is also a validation of the people who had long raised red flags about Agnew's barely concealed bigotry. Early in his vice presidency, when Agnew was accused of stirring up anti-Semitism with his rhetoric and coded language, in particular his speeches against the media, he vehemently denied the accusation. It's hard to look at these private letters from Agnew's later life, though, and come to any other conclusion but that his critics were right about his true sympathies.

During a televised confrontation with NBC's Barbara Walters in 1976, Agnew criticized, at length, what he ominously described as "Zionist influences in the United States." Pressed by Walters about where exactly he believed these influences resided, he responded, "Well, influences certainly in the media . . . [which is] sympathetic to the Zionist cause, put it that way."

Remarks like this caused even some of his closest associates to speak out against him. His longtime friend and speechwriter William Safire wrote a searing op-ed in *The New York Times* more or less accusing his former boss of being an outright anti-Semite. "Hating individual Jews does not make you a bigot," Safire wrote of Agnew. "Being anti-Israel does not make you a bigot. But undertaking a crusade to persuade the American people that they are being brainwashed and manipulated by a cabal of Jews who sit astride most of the channels of communication, and thereby encouraging an irrational hatred of Jews—that makes you a bigot."

Well, yeah. QED.

In May 1995, after years of delay, the U.S. Senate finally commissioned an official marble bust of Spiro T. Agnew to be displayed in the Capitol. Years earlier, when it was noted that Agnew was the only former vice president who had not received the honor, the architect of the Capitol sheepishly admitted that the idea "comes up from time to time," but, he added, "other chores at the Capitol" had pushed aside the decision.

When the bust was finally unveiled, more than a generation after he left office, Agnew himself acknowledged the elephant in the room. "I am not blind or deaf to the fact that there are critics who feel that this is a ceremony that should not take place, that the Senate—by commissioning this bust—is giving me an honor I do not deserve," he said at the ceremony. "I would remind those critics that regardless of their personal view of me, this ceremony has less to do with Spiro Agnew than with the office I held."

Noting with his trademark tinge of bitterness that he had been elected not once but twice, he added, "That fact is part of the fabric of American history. A history that we—as members of a free society—do not alter or obliterate to suit the dogma or the passions of the moment."

Agnew made one other appearance around the same time, which also raised eyebrows: he attended the state funeral of President Richard Nixon.

The two men had spoken not a word to each other after Agnew's unceremonious exit from office. For all the years after, those close to Agnew said, he harbored an extreme bitterness toward President Nixon for failing to rescue him in his time of need.

But when Nixon died in April 1994, Spiro Agnew quietly reached out to one of his daughters, Julie Nixon Eisenhower, and asked whether he would be welcome at the funeral being held at the Nixon Presidential Library. With Julie's blessing, Agnew appeared at the service alongside his wife, Judy.

"I'm here to pay my respects for his accomplishments," Agnew told reporters. "It's time to put aside 20 years of resentment, which is what I'm doing at this moment." He and his wife were seated in the gallery not far from G. Gordon Liddy, a fellow traveler whose time in the Nixon-Agnew White House had also ended in a conviction, though unlike Agnew's his had come with a four-year federal prison sentence.

Agnew himself passed away a little more than two years later on September 17, 1996, while staying at his summer home in Ocean City, Maryland.

The obituary writer in his hometown newspaper, *The Baltimore Sun,* gave Agnew grudging props for having mostly escaped the infamy that was his rightful due. "A life that might easily have become a public misery of disgrace and indebtedness," said the *Sun,* "was instead sheltered and comfortable, with Agnew rarely having to travel in circles where his tarnished reputation mattered. It was a feat he sustained to the very end."

★ ★ ★

HANGING ON THE wall of Marty London's law office in midtown New York City is a newspaper cartoon originally published in October 1973.

The comic, by the artist Paul Conrad, appeared in the *Los Angeles Times* just days after London and his colleagues cut the unprecedented plea deal that kept their famous client out of prison. The black-and-white panel depicts a man in a jail cell, desperately clutching its iron bars. He shouts, "I wanna see Agnew's lawyers!"

Felons across the country may, indeed, have wished they had it as good as the vice president, who secured his freedom by trading his job. But the legacy of what Agnew's lawyers wrought that summer and fall stretches far beyond the terms of that one deal. Their maneuvering led directly to the Justice Department policy, maintained for all the decades since, that a sitting president of the United States cannot be indicted.

It was Agnew's attorneys who argued to the prosecutors from the beginning of August 1973 that their client was immune from prosecution because he was vice president. The Constitution said so, kind of. Their legal Hail

Mary to try to save Agnew touched off a frantic effort inside the Justice Department to grapple with an issue it had
never before confronted. It was in answer to Agnew's attorneys that the Office of Legal Counsel first came to the
not particularly intuitive determination that while a sitting
vice president can be indicted, a sitting *president* cannot.

The Department of Justice also made that argument in
the Agnew case in federal court in Baltimore, in the filing
authored by the then solicitor general, Robert H. Bork: the
vice president is fair game, but the president is immune
from criminal indictment. That argument was a creature
of its time, crafted to answer a remarkable string of circumstances in the early 1970s, when both the president
and the vice president had committed serious criminal
wrongdoing and were each, separately, facing the prospect
of prosecution and/or impeachment with or without their
removal from office. It's also worth noting that at the time
these troubled men were at each other's throats, each one
happy to trade the other's fate to save his own.

The specific proposition of a president's immunity that
was forged in this crucible has never been tested in court,
even though it's frequently cited as if it were binding precedent for all subsequent scandalous presidencies. One influential later solicitor general, Walter Dellinger, says he
doesn't think the original OLC memo, authored by Robert
Dixon, should be the final word. "Robert Dixon was a distinguished lawyer, but it's always been seen by me at least
as a really shoddy piece of work that doesn't explain why,
when there's nothing in the Constitution, you can have a
categorical rule against even indicting a president," Del-

linger says. "Admittedly, you've got to postpone the trial proceedings while he or she is serving.

"But more to the point," he says, "that memo is essentially repudiated nine months later. That September 1973 memo was repudiated when the United States filed in the United States Supreme Court—in the *United States v. Nixon*, by Leon Jaworski, the special counsel, but acting on behalf of the Department of Justice—[and] said they did not accept the proposition that a president could not be indicted." Despite its unusual origins and its weaknesses (and the fact that it's never been tested in court), the 1973 OLC memo still pertains, even to this day, as far as official Department of Justice policy is concerned. And it pertains in very consequential ways. In March 2019, when Special Counsel Robert Mueller declined to charge President Donald Trump with obstruction of justice in relation to his investigation of Russian interference in the 2016 presidential election, Mueller cited the OLC policy initially espoused in the Agnew case as the reason he was unable to even consider an indictment.

"The Office of Legal Counsel (OLC) has issued an opinion finding that 'the indictment or criminal prosecution of a sitting President would impermissibly undermine the capacity of the executive branch to perform its constitutionally assigned functions,'" Mueller wrote in volume 2 of his report, adding that "this Office accepted OLC's legal conclusion" on the matter.

He cited OLC's reasoning again during a press conference. "Under long-standing department policy," he said, "a President cannot be charged with a federal crime while he is in office. That is unconstitutional . . . charging [President Trump] with a crime was, therefore, not an option we could consider."

Spiro T. Agnew and his attorneys didn't save Agnew from prosecution, but they did manage to invent a get-out-of-jail-free card for every criminally corrupt president the future might bring us.

★ ★ ★

WHETHER SPIRO T. AGNEW got the justice he deserved in October 1973 remains, even in the fullness of time, very much in the eye of the beholder.

NBC's David Brinkley made an early stab at defining the meaning of Agnew's historic resignation on the very night it transpired. The son of Greek immigrants, Brinkley noted, Spiro Agnew had risen from county official to vice president in a rags-to-riches tale upended only by Agnew's own greed. "No one knows how many other Washington figures who came up through local politics did the same, and worse," he said, adding, "So, now he leaves and goes back to Baltimore, a tragic and almost pathetic figure."

And that certainly is one way to view Agnew's misdeeds and his ultimate punishment: that he flew too close to the sun and went down in flames. He was not necessarily more corrupt than other politicians; others were just lucky enough not to rise to a high enough position where they were likely to get caught. "I mean, I could sit down with a list of members of Congress in that era," says David Keene, "and list a lot of people that *were* really crooked. By today's standards, what he was accused of wasn't much either."

This particular perspective, with its large strain of in-grown American cynicism, is not shared by a group of men who lived and breathed the Agnew saga in real time: the team of prosecutors in the U.S. Attorney's Office for the District of Maryland. The question of whether "justice" was truly served is pretty obvious to them. "In my view, the answer is very clearly no. He didn't get what he deserved," says Ron Liebman. "What he deserved was to go to trial like any other citizen and, if convicted, to go to jail and have a fine assessed."

Even if the eventual result—Agnew's removal from the line of succession—was the best they could get, what the Department of Justice traded to get him out is still difficult for the prosecutors to accept all these years later.

"He held the office hostage for his own personal bene-fit, and it wasn't his office!" says Tim Baker, nearly five decades later, his voice rising with anger. Agnew's deal still "stings," Baker says. "The office is owned by, it sounds corny, but by the American people. He had no right to sell it, which is what he had done, and he had no right to hold it hostage."

Spiro Agnew probably does deserve to be more infa-mous than he is. His rise and fall barely registers as a foot-note in American history these days; the breadth and details of his venality were never really known by any but a few closer observers. How many people read the forty-page document Skolnik, Liebman, and Baker filed in federal court on the day of Agnew's resignation?

But the federal prosecutors who uncovered his crimes and took him down—they deserve to be more famous than they are. They deserve to be remembered.

U.S. Attorney George Beall, who refused to let pressure from the White House and his own family interfere with his investigation and who valiantly shielded the men working the case, went on to prosecute the next governor of Maryland for corruption, as well: the Democrat Marvin Mandel. He got him, too.

Barney Skolnik and Ron Liebman had a hand in that case. And then, like George Beall, they both moved into quiet careers in private practice.

Tim Baker took over Beall's old job as Maryland U.S. Attorney, ran unsuccessfully for attorney general of Maryland, and then settled into his own career in private practice.

They all ended up doing fine.

But none of them are etched into our history books and our national memory for the crucial role they played in saving the Republic from a criminal vice president ascending to the presidency amid the ashes of Watergate, and quite possibly plunging the country into another unprecedented round of upheaval.

What further damage would have been inflicted on our institutions if we had to remove not one but two presidents back-to-back? These determined government attorneys from Baltimore spared us that disaster, in the face of long odds. Their case was undermined from the White House on down; they were attacked and maligned by the most powerful politicians in the country. Their character

PAUL, WEISS, RIFKIND, WHARTON & GARRISON
345 PARK AVENUE   NEW YORK, N.Y. 10022
TELEPHONE (212) 935-8000
TELECOPIER (212) 935-8302   CABLE LONGSIGHT, N.Y.
                                   TELEX 12-7891

RANDOLPH E. PAUL (1946-1956)   WASHINGTON OFFICE
LOUIS S. WEISS   (1927-1950)   1775 K STREET, N.W.
                                   WASHINGTON, D.C. 20006
JOHN F. WHARTON   TELEPHONE (202) 293-8370
ROBERT S. SAMUELS   CABLE LONGSIGHT WASHINGTON
  COUNSEL

WRITER'S DIRECT DIAL NUMBER   October 19, 1973
(212) 935-8934

The Honorable Elliot L. Richardson
Attorney General of the United States
United States Department of Justice
Washington, D.C.

Dear Elliot:

      Before getting too involved preparing to take other
depositions and negotiating other settlements, I do want to
repeat and amplify what I said to you as you departed Judge
Hoffman's courtroom in Baltimore: your statement to the Court
exemplified your entire approach to this matter; you were both
articulate and honorable and performed a most sensitive task
with grace.

      The next day Jay and I watched your press conference
and both of us made the same appraisal: you were consistent.

      I hope I am not being presumptuous, but it is comfort-
ing to me that the Attorney General of the United States, in
addition to everything else, is a helluva good lawyer (even
though you were on the other side, which, by definition, is
the wrong side). Best regards.

                Sincerely,

                Martin London

A letter from Agnew defense attorney Marty London to Attorney
General Elliot Richardson, in the wake of Richardson's October 11
press conference and on the eve of the Saturday Night Massacre

and their politics were called into question. They endured all of that, at the ripe old average age of about thirty-two. They kept their heads down and they did their jobs.

The bosses in the investigation, Beall and Richardson, led the team without fear or favor, defended the prosecutors themselves and their investigation, and shielded them from the improper pressure they were getting from on high. And then Elliot Richardson forced the deal with Agnew. In doing so, Richardson successfully restored and protected the line of succession, and he did it taking blast-furnace heat from Agnew partisans and Nixon partisans and even his own team of prosecutors.

The day after securing Agnew's resignation, at a Justice Department press conference, a reporter asked Richardson about the lessons the country should take from what it had just witnessed. "I would hope first that the nation would feel that the process of criminal justice is one that it can trust and have confidence in," he began. "I would hope that, most fundamentally, all of us would have confidence that our system works. Indeed, I think this is the most affirmative aspect of all that has taken place over recent months—all the disclosures, the investigations, the indictments—they have exposed the shoddy side of the governmental and political process, but they have also demonstrated that the governmental and political process is capable of uncovering these things, and—having uncovered them—taking proper action."

Elliot Richardson served in a variety of posts in the Gerald Ford administration, but never again in one with the stature or import of attorney general. His five months of

From left: Ron Liebman, Tim Baker, George Beall, and Barney Skolnik, outside the Baltimore federal courthouse

running the Department of Justice in 1973 was the high-light of his career. When he returned to the Justice Depart-ment on the first Monday after he had resigned on principle in the Saturday Night Massacre, he never forgot the thun-derous and sustained ovation he received from the men and women who had served under him.

Richardson died of a cerebral hemorrhage on Decem-ber 31, 1999. He didn't quite make it to the twenty-first century, but he can take credit for helping to steer the ship of state safely there.

George Beall died in January 2017, just days before the inauguration of the nation's newest president, Donald Trump. One of his successors as U.S. Attorney in Mary-land put out a statement honoring Beall's career as a gov-ernment prosecutor. Unsurprisingly, the focus was on one particular case.

"George Beall was a legendary federal prosecutor, an exemplary public servant and a lawyer of unsurpassed in-tegrity," the statement read. "Although George Beall's fam-ily was politically active and Vice President Agnew was a member of Beall's own political party, Beall did not hesi-tate to pursue the case. His commitment to justice serves as an example to us all."

That statement—about a public servant having the courage to pursue a popular elected official, no matter the shared party affiliation—was written by the then Maryland U.S. Attorney, Rod Rosenstein, who just weeks later would be appointed deputy attorney general of the United States, by Donald Trump, a position that would put him in charge of overseeing the special counsel investigation into Trump and his campaign.

George Beall didn't often speak publicly about the events of 1973, but he later described it as "a very lonely time" in his life. At the age of thirty-five, with his entire political career ahead of him, he had not shied when he faced the prospect of taking on the second most powerful man in the country. The effort surely did great damage to his political future in the Republican Party. The spotlight at the time of the battle was intense, Beall would remember, but he and his team "did what we were duty-bound to do. And that is to enforce the law against every person, no matter how high in rank or public office."

"If I leave this office without enemies, I will not have done the job properly," Beall said. "I think that the public has to know there is an office somewhere that is incorruptible."

★ ★ ★

ACKNOWLEDGMENTS

Thank you, thank you to all of the smart, hardworking folks at Crown whose patience and persistence helped us bring this book into the world. Especially Gillian Blake, Caroline Wray, Meghan Houser, and David Drake.

Thanks to the absolutely indispensable Mark Zwonitzer for all of his tireless efforts. And to Laurie Liss for moving all of the parts necessary to make this book a reality.

Special thanks to the bosses at MSNBC and NBC News, in particular Phil Griffin and Elisabeth Sami, who took a leap of faith in believing us that a forty-five-year-old story about Spiro T. Agnew really *did* need to be told. At length! And right now.

Thanks also to the great and good staff of *The Rachel Maddow Show,* whose patience and forbearance know no bounds.

Most of all, thanks to those who lived this history and who were generous enough with their time to let us interview them about it: Martin London, J. T. Smith, John Banzhaf, David Keene.

And most especially: Barney Skolnik, Tim Baker, and Ron Liebman, the dogged Baltimore federal prosecutors whose efforts—quite literally—helped save this country from absolute catastrophe. We all owe them a debt of gratitude. And their dedicated public service ought to be remembered by history.

★ ★ ★

A NOTE ON SOURCES

*B*ag *Man* is the product of hours of sit-down interviews
with many of those directly involved in the Agnew
case, historical research conducted at archives and libraries across the country, and original reporting.

Our primary research sites were the Richard Nixon
Presidential Library and Museum in Yorba Linda, California; the Spiro T. Agnew Papers held at the University of
Maryland in College Park; the papers of Elliot L. Richardson held at the Library of Congress in Washington, D.C.;
and the papers of the U.S. Attorney George Beall held at
Frostburg State University in Maryland.

The documents we relied upon included personal correspondence, handwritten notes from key meetings, calendars and schedules, official memos to file from the
investigation, and audio recordings made by, among others, President Richard Nixon and the White House chief of
staff H. R. Haldeman. (Although the Nixon tapes are well
known, the Haldeman audio diaries remain an underap-
preciated historical resource, and they're fascinating on

their own terms; you can find the transcripts and high-quality audio files on the website of the Nixon Library.) Where specific documents from archives and libraries have been used in the book, the citations in the pages that follow note their origins.

In general, direct quotations in the text are drawn from in-person interviews conducted originally for the *Bag Man* podcast. Those interviews—with the Baltimore prosecutors, Agnew's defense attorney Marty London, David Keene, and others—are not cited in the pages that follow, but where a quotation comes from a non-interview source (such as a historical document or a contemporaneous news report), this is noted.

The research for this book also relied heavily upon archival television news reports, primarily from NBC News, contemporaneous newspaper and magazine coverage, and published works, including the personal memoirs and autobiographies of those involved. Of the books on the subject, none are more complete than *A Heartbeat Away*, by the *Washington Post* reporters Richard Cohen and Jules Witcover, published a year after the investigation concluded. Where information was derived from any of these sources, it is also noted in the following section.

Additional documents were provided to us by the collector Gregg Schneider. These include personal papers of Spiro Agnew that shed light on the decades-long business and consulting career that followed his felony plea and resignation from office. Our thanks to Gregg for making those papers available to us; they were essential in supplementing the material that is publicly available.

And particular thanks to the archivists, librarians, and researchers at the institutions and libraries mentioned above whose knowledge and expertise were invaluable and without whom this story could not have been told. You guys are a national treasure.

★ ★ ★

NOTES

PROLOGUE: "WHAT'S A SPIRO AGNEW?"

4   **"to do what Asian boys"** "GOP Viet Views," *Los Angeles Times*, Sept. 20, 1966.

4   **"pain [the war] has inflicted"** Lyndon Johnson, national address, Washington, D.C., March 31, 1968.

7   **"We should side with Daley"** Patrick Buchanan, "With Nixon in '68: The Year America Came Apart," *Wall Street Journal*, April 5, 2018.

8   **"when the looting starts"** "Curfew Slapped on Most of City," *Miami News*, Aug. 9, 1968.

8   **"clouds of tear gas"** "Riots Spread, Then Cool," *Miami News*, Aug. 9, 1968.

8   **"I'd do it again"** "Cop Tells Why He Used Gas," *Miami News*, Aug. 13, 1968.

9   **"Just think how much"** Richard Nixon, press conference, Los Angeles, Nov. 7, 1962.

10   **"Our deliberations took place"** Richard Nixon, press conference, Miami, Fla., Aug. 8, 1968.

11   **"I think the best indication"** Richard Nixon, remarks to press, Miami, Fla., NBC News, Aug. 8, 1968.

11 **"What's a Spiro Agnew?"** Erma Bombeck, "Think You're So Smart: What's a Spiro Agnew?," *Boston Globe*, Dec. 3, 1968.

13 *"My kind of man"* Spiro T. Agnew 1966 gubernatorial campaign radio ads, Richard Nixon Presidential Library and Museum, Yorba Linda, Calif.

14 **man's laughter grows louder** Hubert Humphrey 1968 presidential campaign television ad, "Laughter," Museum of the Moving Image.

15 **"I'll tell you this"** "Agnew Lashes Out at Anti-war Demonstrators," *Poughkeepsie Journal*, Sept. 6, 1968.

15 **"Somewhere, somebody failed you"** Spiro T. Agnew, 1968 presidential campaign, NBC News Archives.

15 **"the officer should not hesitate"** "Fleeing Looters Should Be Shot, Agnew Asserts," *Cumberland News* (Cumberland, Md.), Aug. 2, 1968.

15 **"would be a tremendous deterrent"** "I'm No Looter-Shooter: Agnew," *New York Daily News*, Aug. 10, 1968.

15 **During one short stretch** "Agnew Campaign Hawaii Racial Slurs," *NBC Nightly News*, Sept. 24, 1968.

16 **"the boo-boo in a muu-muu"** "Agnew Took Rough Road to VP," *Baltimore Sun*, Sept. 9, 2000.

16 **"I guess by nature"** "HHH Has Been a Softy, Agnew Says," *Detroit Free Press*, Sept. 11, 1968.

16 **"In Spiro Agnew"** Patrick J. Buchanan, *Nixon's White House Wars: The Battles That Made and Broke a President and Divided America Forever* (New York: Crown Forum, 2017), 97.

CHAPTER I: DIVIDER IN CHIEF

20 *"NBC interrupts its regular"* NBC News Special Report, April 4, 1968.

21 **"Martin Luther King dedicated his life"** Robert F. Kennedy, speech in Indianapolis, April 4, 1968, John F. Kennedy Presidential Library and Museum.

22 **Agnew ordered more than** "Agnew Wires Johnson; 'Insurrection' Spills to Slums on West Side," *Baltimore Sun,* April 8, 1968.

23 **Agnew filibustered from the start** Governor Spiro T. Agnew, "Statement at Conference with Civil Rights Leaders and Community Leaders, State Office Building," April 11, 1968, Maryland State Archives.

23 **"He is as sick as any bigot"** "Many Blacks Walked Out on Agnew's Angry Talk," *Baltimore Evening Sun,* June 23, 1970.

24 **"Agnew had called in"** Buchanan, C-SPAN interview, Feb. 13, 2012.

27 **"You know how it is with the radical liberals"** Spiro Agnew, speech in Hartford, Oct. 23, 1970, NBC News Archives.

27 **During one post-election stop** Spiro Agnew, speech in Springfield, Ill., Sept. 10, 1970, NBC News Archives.

28 **"Agnew told me years ago"** John R. Coyne Jr., "Buchanan on Nixon: Triumph and Tragedy," *American Conservative,* May 4, 2017.

28 **"He was asked why he"** David Brinkley, *NBC Nightly News,* Jan. 3, 1971.

29 **"Enthusiasm for Agnew's knock-heads"** "Don't Get Agnew Wrong," *Life,* May 8, 1970.

29 **"He said what a lot of us"** Ibid.

29 **"[He] is seriously ill"** Associated Press, "Ford Demands Negro Apologize to Agnew," *Tampa Tribune,* July 23, 1971.

30 **A confidential source informed the FBI** Memo from FBI to U.S. Secret Service, "Alleged Plot to Assassinate Vice President Agnew," Oct. 6, 1970, FBI FOIA docs.

30 **"I'd brought a tab of LSD"** John Henry Browne, *The Devil's Defender: My Odyssey Through American Criminal Justice from Ted Bundy to the Kandahar Massacre* (Chicago: Chicago Review Press, 2016).

32 **"As he quietly read"** Buchanan, *Nixon's White House Wars,* 70.

32 **he pitted average Americans** Spiro Agnew, speech in Des Moines, Nov. 13, 1969, NBC News Archives.

32 **"What do Americans know"** Ibid.

33 **"I think the networks deserve"** "New FCC Chief Backs Agnew's Charge," *Shreveport (La.) Times,* Nov. 15, 1969.

33 **"a matter of immense importance"** "Agnew Relaxes Attack on Media," *New York Times,* April 13, 1973.

33 **Seemingly following Agnew's lead** "New FCC Chief Backs Agnew's Charge."

34 **The president of NBC News appeared** Commentary by NBC News president Julian Goodman, *NBC Nightly News,* Nov. 14, 1969.

34 **an attempt to bring newspapers** Associated Press, "Newspapers and TV Called Targets of Nixon Drive," *Los Angeles Times,* Nov. 20, 1969.

34 **"I'm not out to vilify"** Spiro Agnew, speech in Montgomery, Ala., Nov. 21, 1969, NBC News Archives.

34 **"One little noted and wholly unintentional"** "Agnew Unintentionally Triggers Renewed Round of Anti-Semitism," *Washington Post,* Dec. 30, 1969.

35 **"I've always lived by my instincts"** "Don't Get Agnew Wrong."

36 **Judy Agnew appeared both ecstatic and relieved** Vice President Agnew and Judy Agnew, interview, *NBC News Special Report,* Jan. 20, 1973.

CHAPTER 2: FOLLOW THE MONEY

37 **He rushed to the horse barn** "Rep. Mills Found Shot to Death," *Salisbury (Md.) Daily Times,* May 24, 1973.

38 **"I've done nothing wrong"** UPI, "Dead Congressman's Notes Kept Secret," *Philadelphia Daily News*, May 25, 1973.

39 **"This rotten vine of Watergate"** "3 Top Nixon Aides, Kleindienst Out; President Accepts Full Responsibility; Richardson Will Conduct New Probe," *Washington Post*, May 1, 1973.

39 **"Whatever else I shall be"** "Cox Is Chosen as Special Prosecutor," *Washington Post*, May 19, 1973.

40 **Records showed the Mills congressional campaign** Associated Press, "Rep. Mills Says Role Proper in Campaign Gift," *Salisbury (Md.) Daily Times*, May 23, 1973.

41 **Notorious dens of political corruption** "Gallery of Maryland Officials Involved in Corruption," *Washington Post*, Aug. 25, 1977.

41 **when one county official was convicted** "Joseph Alton, First Anne Arundel Executive, Dies," *Capital Gazette* (Annapolis, Md.), March 30, 2013.

43 **"The difference between Maryland"** "Maryland's Political Trials," *Washington Post*, Aug. 25, 1977.

44 **"Rule one"** "Closing In on Agnew: The Prosecutors' Story," *New York*, Nov. 26, 1973.

46 **the blaring headline** "Subpoenas Catch Baltimore County Off Guard," *Baltimore Sun*, Jan. 10, 1973.

CHAPTER 3: JUST BEING CAREFUL

52 **"In the past this office"** Beall to Johnnie M. Walters (IRS commissioner), March 2, 1972, Beall Collection, Frostburg State University, Frostburg, Md.

53 **The reason Kleindienst was pressing** Memorandum from Beall to Baltimore County File, July 25, 1973, Beall Collection.

55 **personal phone call from the prosecutor Tim Baker** Memorandum from Baker to Baltimore County File, April 13, 1973, Beall Collection.

58 **"I give you the tools"** "Congress Clears 1970 Organized Crime Control Bill," *CQ Almanac 1970*, 26th ed.; "Nixon Signs Bills to Combat Crime," *New York Times*, Oct. 16, 1970.

60 **Lester Matz himself opened a line** Richard Cohen and Jules Witcover, *A Heartbeat Away* (New York: Viking Press, 1974), 80–81.

61 **"very concerned about the national implications"** Memorandum from Baker to Baltimore County File, May 21, 1973, Beall Collection.

61 **Kaplan remained frustratingly noncommittal** Memorandum from Baker to Baltimore County File, May 18, 1973, Beall Collection.

CHAPTER 4: "OTHERWISE DECENT"

64 **Matz's luck changed** "Exposition of the Evidence Against Spiro T. Agnew," Department of Justice, Oct. 10, 1973, Federal Records in the National Archives of the United States.

64 **Agnew asked Matz to draw up** Ibid.

66 **He personally handed Agnew the cash** Memorandum from Baker to Baltimore County File, June 22, 1973, Beall Collection.

68 **Each time secretly handing** Ibid.

68 **Secret Service logs** U.S. Secret Service Appointment Records, Visits by Lester Matz to Vice President Agnew, Spiro T. Agnew Papers, Special Collections, University of Maryland Libraries.

69 **turned up a similar arrangement** "Exposition of the Evidence Against Spiro T. Agnew."

70 **The White House logs confirmed** U.S. Secret Service Appointment Records for Lester Matz, Bud Hammerman, and Allen Green, Agnew Papers.

71 **Ehrlichman was stunned** John Ehrlichman, *Witness to Power* (New York: Simon & Schuster, 1982), 143.

71 **Agnew got word to Lester Matz** "Exposition of the Evidence Against Spiro T. Agnew."

CHAPTER 5: "OH MY GOD"

76 **During an emotional meeting at Camp David** Elliot L. Richardson, *The Creative Balance: Government, Politics, and the Individual in America's Third Century* (New York: Holt, Rinehart and Winston, 1976), 4.

77 **"It is my honest belief"** John W. Dean III, testimony before the U.S. Senate Select Committee on Presidential Campaign Activities, June 25, 1973.

82 **"he was greatly concerned for the nation"** Memorandum from Baker to Baltimore County File, July 5, 1973, Beall Collection.

CHAPTER 6: THE PRUDENT COURSE

84 **Nixon had reportedly asked his aides** "Nixon Hospitalized," *New York Times*, July 15, 1973.

85 **"I've been blessed with"** "State of Nixon's Health Is a Dimension of Watergate Affair Constantly Being Gauged," *New York Times*, Dec. 4, 1973.

85 **"[Nixon's] skin was pasty"** Alexander Haig, *Inner Circles: How America Changed the World: A Memoir* (New York: Warner Books, 1992), 371.

85 **Nixon ended up hospitalized** *NBC Nightly News*, July 15, 1973.

88 **"You won't lose by it"** "Exposition of the Evidence Against Spiro T. Agnew."

89 **"Over the course of"** Ibid.

90 **Agnew settled on this** Ibid.

91 **Wolff had turned all of these notebooks** Report of Laboratory Examination of Jerome B. Wolff Pocket Diary, Bureau of Alcohol, Tobacco, and Firearms, Sept. 14, 1973, Beall Collection.

93 **"Have you intentionally given the Government"** FBI Memos from Baltimore County Investigation Polygraph Examinations, Aug. 13, 1973, FBI FOIA Files on Spiro Agnew Investigation, File Number 58-8211.

94 **"my guy is hopping up and down"** Memorandum from Beall to Baltimore County File, July 18, 1973, Beall Collection.

94 **"This office is now conducting"** Beall to Best, Aug. 1, 1973, Beall Collection.

98 **According to handwritten notes** Notes on meeting between President Richard Nixon and Attorney General Elliot Richardson, Aug. 5, 1973, Nixon Presidential Library and Museum.

98 **"I told the Vice President"** Memorandum for the file by Attorney General Elliot Richardson, Aug. 14, 1973, Elliot L. Richardson Papers, Manuscript Division, Library of Congress, Washington, D.C.

100 **"You're going to be sorry"** "How Agnew Bartered His Office to Keep from Going to Prison," *New York Times*, Oct. 23, 1973.

CHAPTER 7: "I HAVE NO INTENTION TO BE SKEWERED
IN THIS FASHION"

102 **"Vice President Spiro T. Agnew"** "Agnew Investigated in Extortion Case," *Wall Street Journal*, Aug. 7, 1973.

102 *The Washington Post* **was right behind** "Agnew Under U.S. Probe for Bribery, Conspiracy," *Washington Post*, Aug. 7, 1973.

102 **"Washington was stunned today"** John Chancellor, *NBC Nightly News*, Aug. 7, 1973.

103 **"I strongly suggest that, if at all possible"** Memo from Skolnik to Beall, "Miscellaneous Thoughts for the Team to Ponder While I Am on Vacation," Aug. 24, 1973, Beall Collection.

104 **"Because of defamatory statements"** Spiro T. Agnew, statement to the press, Aug. 8, 1973.

105 **"That was one hell of a press conference"** Memo from Buchanan to Agnew, Aug. 8, 1973, Agnew Papers.

105 **Agnew fired off a response** Memo from Agnew to Buchanan, Aug. 15, 1973, Agnew Papers.

105 **hundreds of letters** Letters to Vice President Agnew from supporters, Agnew Papers.

106 **"The man has been put under"** Buckley and Dole, interview, 1973, NBC News Archives.

107 **"To condemn someone"** Curtis, interview, Sept. 19, 1973, NBC News Archives.

107 **began to fill up with mail** Letters to Attorney General Richardson, Richardson Papers.

108 **"Despite all the Vice President's protestations"** "Heading Toward an Indictment?," *Time*, Aug. 27, 1973.

108 **"persons involved in the investigatory process"** Spiro T. Agnew, statement to the press, Aug. 21, 1973.

109 **"I will say this"** President Richard M. Nixon, remarks to the press, San Clemente, Calif., Aug. 22, 1973.

109 **"I have today asked"** "Richardson Discloses an Inquiry on Justice Leaks About Agnew," *New York Times*, Aug. 23, 1973.

CHAPTER 8: "IS HE A GOOD BOY?"

110 **"Have you made comments to anyone"** Sworn statement of George Beall, Oct. 5, 1973, Beall Collection.

112 **"His voice was strained"** Spiro T. Agnew, *Go Quietly . . . or Else* (New York: William Morrow, 1980), 41.

114 **"The Vice President called me over today"** April 10, 1973, entry, H. R. Haldeman Diaries Collection, Nixon Presidential Library and Museum.

116 **"Did Bob [Haldeman] tell you about"** Conversation on April 13, 1973, Richard Nixon White House Tapes, Nixon Presidential Library and Museum.

118 **"Can you imagine a guy"** Conversation on June 14, 1973, Nixon White House Tapes.

122 **Nixon and Agnew personally helped** "Nixon Visits Baltimore, Hails Beall," *Baltimore Sun*, Oct. 25, 1970; "Beall Feted by Agnew at Republican Dinner," *Baltimore Evening Sun*, Oct. 21, 1970.

124 **Nixon wrote in his memoir** Richard Nixon, *RN: The Memoirs of Richard Nixon* (New York: Simon & Schuster, 1990), 816.

125 **"I want to get Mel"** Conversation on June 19, 1973, Nixon White House Tapes.

127 **"The Vice President has been very nervous"** Conversation on June 20, 1973, Nixon White House Tapes.

128 **"With respect to conversations"** Memorandum from Beall to Baltimore County File, July 25, 1973, Beall Collection.

128 **Bush's personal diaries** "Bush's Diaries on Iran-Contra Made Public," *St. Louis Post-Dispatch*, Jan. 16, 1993.

128 **Bush unexpectedly pardoned** "Bush Pardons Six in Iran Affair," *New York Times*, Dec. 24, 1992.

129 **Agnew personally lobbied Senator Beall** Vice President Spiro T. Agnew, Notes & Daily Calendars, 1973, Agnew Papers.

132 **George Beall wrote in his files** Memorandum from Beall to Baltimore County File, July 25, 1973, Beall Collection.

CHAPTER 9: "HIGH-RISK BALL"

135 **A raging monsoon** "Agnew Is Forced to Drop Korean Visit with Troops," *Louisville (Ky.) Courier-Journal*, July 3, 1971.

135 **Morocco turned into** Associated Press, "Scars of Coup
Visible as Agnew Visits Morocco," *Arizona Republic,*
July 25, 1971.

135 **The Kuwait leg was marred** "Agnew Kuwait Visit Marred
by Row," *Baltimore Evening Sun,* July 7, 1971.

135 **"After viewing the adventure"** "Agnew Junket Hoax on
the People," *Decatur (Ill.) Daily Review,* July 8, 1971.

136 **On arrival in Nairobi** Associated Press, "Agnew Tries
Out Kenya Golf Links," *Statesman Journal* (Salem, Ore.),
July 13, 1971.

136 **During his swing through Spain** UPI, "Agnew Takes Golf
Break, China Speculation Rife," *Oakland Tribune,* July 19,
1971.

136 **limited time in Morocco** Associated Press, "Agnew Takes
Golf Break, Visits with King Hassan," *Corpus Christi
(Tex.) Caller-Times,* July 25, 1971.

136 **"utter stupidity"** Conversation on July 20, 1971, Nixon
White House Tapes.

136 **"He played golf every damn day!"** Conversation on July 28,
1971, Nixon White House Tapes.

138 **If he had behaved that way** Conversation on May 17, 1973,
Nixon White House Tapes.

138 **"I was never allowed to come close"** Agnew, *Go Quietly . . .
or Else,* 34.

138 **Nixon called the White House counsel** Conversation on
April 7, 1971, Nixon White House Tapes.

139 **"[Nixon] enumerated some of"** July 20, 1971, entry, Haldeman Diaries Collection.

139 **He was getting fond of** Conversation on April 7, 1971,
Nixon White House Tapes.

140 **seen it enormously upgraded** "Money, Money, Money,"
New York Times, Jan. 13, 1974.

140 *Lawrence of Arabia* Presidential daily diary of Aug. 24 and 25, 1973, Nixon Presidential Library and Museum.

141 **"presided over what many believed"** "The Future Years: But Only Events Can Settle the Biggest Question of All," *New York Times,* Aug. 26, 1973.

142 **"Watergate is an episode"** President Richard M. Nixon, remarks to the press, San Clemente, Calif., Aug. 22, 1973.

142 **"Getting to the truth"** "Desperate Hours," *New York Times,* Aug. 26, 1973.

143 **Nixon administration had wiretapped** "3 High U.S. Aides Reported Target of Taps in 1969–71," *New York Times,* Aug. 25, 1973.

143 **"Nixon was aware of the whole"** UPI, "Nixon Knew All About Coverup, Martha Says," *Los Angeles Times,* Aug. 26, 1973.

144 **Coopers & Lybrand accounting firm** "Text of Letter from Auditors to President on Acquisition of His Properties," *New York Times,* Aug. 27, 1973.

144 **"A viper sleeping in bed"** Patrick Buchanan, "Deep State Appears Determined to Take Down President Trump," *Sioux City (Iowa) Journal,* May 18, 2017.

145 **"In all candor"** "A Historic Ruling: President First Since Jefferson Directed to Give Up Records," *New York Times,* Aug. 30, 1973.

146 **"I don't even contemplate"** "Nixon Flies Back from the Coast for Agnew Talk," *New York Times,* Sept. 1, 1973.

146 **"I had confidence in the integrity"** President Richard M. Nixon, remarks to the press, San Clemente, Calif., Aug. 22, 1973.

146 **Nixon's bar for integrity** Excerpts from David Frost's fourth interview with former president Nixon, "'I'm Not Going to Sit Here and Judge Spiro Agnew,'" *Washington Post,* May 26, 1977.

149 **"liable to prosecution and punishment"** "Agnew Suddenly Shares in Nixon Legal Dilemma," *New York Times*, Aug. 9, 1973.

150 **"The best solution"** Haig, *Inner Circles*, 356.

150 **He was being railroaded** Agnew, *Go Quietly . . . or Else*, 143.

150 **"You'll be playing high-risk ball"** Ibid., 142.

151 **"I'll fight this"** Ibid., 146.

151 **"did not have the stomach"** Ibid., 104.

CHAPTER 10: "TWO CONDITIONS"

153 **"I had turned over a log"** Richardson, *Creative Balance*, 101.

154 **"We now believe that the following offenses"** Memorandum from U.S. Attorney George Beall for Attorney General Elliot Richardson, "Status Report on the Investigation of Vice President Agnew and Others," Sept. 11, 1973, Beall Collection.

156 **"We are about to embark"** "Closing In on Agnew."

157 **According to George Beall's notes** Memorandum by U.S. Attorney George Beall, "Meeting with Counsel for the Vice President," Sept. 19, 1973, National Archives of the United States.

162 **"Once we get his problem"** "Closing In on Agnew."

163 **A strategy memo suggested** Richard Nixon White House Central Files (1969–1974), Nixon Presidential Library and Museum.

163 **"Some high White House officials"** "Some Nixon Aides Hint That Agnew Ought to Resign," *New York Times*, Sept. 19, 1973.

164 **"Here's how it went"** Tom Brokaw, *NBC Nightly News*, Sept. 18, 1973.

164 **"You must do what is best"** Agnew, *Go Quietly . . . or Else,* 158.

164 **"I don't give a damn"** "Federal Jury Launches Investigation of Agnew," *Arizona Daily Star,* Sept. 28, 1973.

165 **Front-page large-type headlines** "Agnew Is Reported in Plea-Bargaining," *Philadelphia Inquirer,* Sept. 22, 1973; "Agnew Reported to Be Bargaining for Lighter Charge," *Minneapolis Star,* Sept. 22, 1973; "Agnew Reported Resigning as 'Plea Bargain,'" *Cincinnati Enquirer,* Sept. 22, 1973.

165 **"We've got the evidence"** "The Petersen Case," *New York Times,* Oct. 1, 1973.

166 **"They'd have to dynamite him"** Gold, interview, Sept. 18, 1973, NBC News Archives.

166 **"I'm innocent"** "How Agnew Bartered His Office to Keep from Going to Prison."

CHAPTER II: IN HIS TIME OF GREATEST NEED

168 **The night of his inauguration** "Frank Had a Ball and JFK Came," *Miami News,* Jan. 21, 1961.

169 **"From the beginning"** Agnew, *Go Quietly . . . or Else,* 191, 204.

169 **"I had heard all this garbage"** Ibid., 205.

169 **Sinatra's friends were willing** "Sinatra Reported Working Hard Among Friends to Raise Money to Aid Agnew," *New York Times,* Dec. 4, 1973.

169 **"I met a lot of celebrities"** Agnew, *Go Quietly . . . or Else,* 177.

171 **The OLC trawled through** "Amenability of the President, Vice President, and Other Civil Officers to Federal Criminal Prosecution While in Office," Office of Legal Counsel Memorandum, Assistant Attorney General Robert G. Dixon Jr., Sept. 24, 1973.

177 **"Petersen, in his very detached way"** Excerpts from Frost's fourth interview with Nixon, "'I'm Not Going to Sit Here and Judge Spiro Agnew.'"

CHAPTER 12: "I'M A BIG TROPHY"

179 **Sporting a conservative dark gray suit** "Agnew's Lawyers and Justice Dept. Reach an Impasse," *New York Times,* Sept. 26, 1973.

180 **"I respectfully request"** Agnew to Albert, Sept. 25, 1973, Agnew Papers.

181 **"Nothing's ruled out"** "Agnew's Lawyers and Justice Dept. Reach an Impasse."

181 **Agnew filed a motion** "Agnew Bids Court Bar Investigation by Federal Jury," *New York Times,* Sept. 29, 1973.

182 **The two pals got in a game** Justin P. Coffey, *Spiro Agnew and the Rise of the Republican Right* (Santa Barbara, Calif.: Praeger, 2015), 189.

183 **At breakfast the next morning** "Agnew Loosed Attack After Weeks of Anger," *New York Times,* Oct. 1, 1973.

183 **"they're supporting him"** Catherine Mackin, *NBC News Special Report,* Sept. 29, 1973.

183 **"Some women approached newsmen"** "GOP Women Still Resent Press," *Troy (N.Y.) Times Record,* Oct. 2, 1973.

184 **"I don't know what it is"** "Agnew Loosed Attack After Weeks of Anger."

184 **"In the past several months"** Spiro T. Agnew, speech to National Federation of Republican Women, Los Angeles, Sept. 29, 1973, NBC News Archives.

187 **"Yelling and waving anything"** "Agnew Declares He Will Not Quit; Attacks Inquiry," *New York Times,* Sept. 30, 1973.

CHAPTER 13: SUBPOENA ENVY

188 **"The Vice President has singled out"** Statement from Attorney General Elliot L. Richardson, Sept. 29, 1973, Beall Collection.

192 **The imposing judge famously** "Agnew Case Boosts 'Beef' Hoffman into Prominence," *New York Times,* Sept. 30, 1973.

192 **"It is because I have learned"** Judge Walter E. Hoffman, Transcript of Supplemental Charge to Grand Jury, Baltimore, Oct. 3, 1973.

193 **The document London presented** "Reporters' Counsel Meet on Strategy for Agnew Inquiry," *New York Times,* Oct. 8, 1973.

196 **"Let's see if [Judge Hoffman]"** Ben Bradlee, *A Good Life: Newspapering and Other Adventures* (New York: Simon & Schuster, 1995), 365.

196 **"not going to disclose"** John Chancellor, *NBC Nightly News,* Oct. 5, 1973.

196 **"Whether or not [Agnew's] lawyers"** David Brinkley commentary, *NBC Nightly News,* Oct. 5, 1973.

197 **Solicitor General Robert H. Bork** "Memorandum for the United States Concerning the Vice President's Claim of Constitutional Immunity" (filed Oct. 5, 1973), In re Proceedings of the Grand Jury Impaneled December 5, 1972: Application of Spiro T. Agnew, Vice President of the United States (D. Md. 1973) (No. 73-965).

CHAPTER 14: "WE'RE GOING TO BE CRITICIZED FOR WHAT WE DO HERE TODAY"

202 **"This man is the goddamn vice president"** "Closing In on Agnew."

202 **"Attorney General Richardson was persuaded"** George Beall, speech at Frostburg State University, Sept. 30, 2003.

207 **They got it there, in fact, five minutes late** Cohen and Witcover, *Heartbeat Away,* 336.

210 **And then the historic proceedings began** Transcript of Spiro T. Agnew Trial Proceedings, Baltimore, Oct. 10, 1973.

213 **"I categorically and flatly deny"** Spiro T. Agnew, remarks to the press, Baltimore, Oct. 10, 1973, NBC News Archives.

214 **"There was disbelief on Capitol Hill"** NBC News correspondent Paul Duke, *NBC News Special Report*, Oct. 10, 1973.

214 **"I'm just sick about it"** Interviews with Spiro Agnew supporters, Oct. 1973, NBC News Archives.

216 **"the most serious constitutional crisis"** John Chancellor, *NBC News Special Report*, Oct. 20, 1973.

CHAPTER 15: WHY'D HE DO IT?

218 **"Lightning kept striking this guy"** "Agnew's Meteoric Career Began Brightly in MD," *Washington Post*, Sept. 19, 1996.

219 **"sent a chill through my body"** Agnew, *Go Quietly . . . or Else*, 189.

220 **according to Dunn's memorialization** Ibid., 187–89.

220 **"I didn't know what General Haig meant"** Agnew, interview, 1980, KABC-TV, Los Angeles.

221 **Agnew said that he was so fearful** Agnew, interview, *Meet the Press*, NBC, May 18, 1980.

221 **"I've never said it was"** Ibid.

222 **"was the most preposterous thing"** "Agnew: I Quit Because I Feared for My Life," *Washington Post*, April 20, 1980.

224 **Agnew was so concerned** Nixon, *RN*, 915.

CHAPTER 16: DISAPPEARING ACT

225 **"What we are about to see"** John Chancellor, *NBC News Special Report*, Oct. 15, 1973.

226 **"I do not want to spend"** Spiro T. Agnew, speech from NBC News studios, Washington, D.C., Oct. 15, 1973, NBC News Archives.

228 **After his speech that night** UPI, "Agnew Speech Greeted with Disbelief, Sarcasm," *Lincoln (Neb.) Journal Star*, Oct. 16, 1973.

228 **"so that my vice-presidential papers"** Agnew, *Go Quietly . . . or Else,* 149.

230 **"He still comes downtown almost daily"** "Letdown Marks Shift to Citizen Agnew," *Baltimore Sun,* Nov. 6, 1973.

230 **When he visited his devoted pal** "Agnew and Sinatra Visit Here; Have No Comment on Anything," *Chicago Tribune,* Oct. 27, 1973.

230 **"I'm here to relax"** Associated Press, "Spiro and Frank Enjoying Life," *Missoulian* (Missoula, Mont.), Oct. 28, 1973.

230 **"It probably is the first time"** "Secret Service Protects Felon," *Chicago Sun-Times/Raleigh (N.C.) Register,* Oct. 29, 1973.

230 **"How long the agents"** "Guards for Agnew," *Munster (Ind.) Times,* Oct. 31, 1973.

230 **Letters from sympathetic supporters** Agnew correspondence with supporters, Oct. 29 and Dec. 5, 1973, Agnew Papers.

231 **When Agnew arrived in California** "Agnew, Guest of Sinatra, Guarded by U.S. Agents," *Los Angeles Times,* Feb. 14, 1974.

232 **"This is an outrageous act"** "Guard for Agnew Assailed," *Cincinnati Enquirer,* Feb. 14, 1974.

232 **"Suddenly one evening"** Agnew, *Go Quietly . . . or Else,* 149.

232 **"I needed one thing urgently"** Ibid., 219.

233 **the couple swung through Washington** "Sinatra Reported Working Hard Among Friends to Raise Money to Aid Agnew."

233 **Agnew wasn't a good fit** "Agnew Loses Job Offer," *Lincoln (Neb.) Journal Star,* Jan. 6, 1974.

233 **"I resigned to save [Jameson]"** Agnew, *Go Quietly . . . or Else,* 203.

234 **The Department of State received a cable** U.S. State Department cable, "The Veep Connection—Messrs. Agnew and Sinatra Reportedly Here," Nov. 30, 1973, released by WikiLeaks.

234 **brief flurry of speculation** "Agnew, Sinatra Venture?," *Palm Beach Post* (West Palm Beach, Fla.), Oct. 28, 1973.

235 **"extreme inventiveness"** John Kenneth Galbraith, "The Canfield Decision," *New York Times,* June 6, 1976.

235 **The book was widely panned** "A Mean-Spirited Piece of Work," *Rochester (N.Y.) Democrat and Chronicle/Newsday,* May 23, 1976.

235 **The book was rife** "Agnew's Apology Settles Defamation Suit," *Washington Post,* June 14, 1981.

236 **"I hope you will accept"** Ibid.

236 **"White interrogated me"** Agnew, *Go Quietly . . . or Else,* 43.

240 **"a chance for the little guys"** "Taxpayer, Activist Anger, Sachs's Switch Led to Victory in Agnew Lawsuit," *Baltimore Sun,* April 30, 1981.

241 **"It's been going on for a thousand years"** "Spiro T. Agnew's Longtime Friend and Attorney George White . . . ," UPI, April 24, 1981.

242 **"I was under oath"** Interview of George White, *NBC Nightly News,* April 24, 1981.

EPILOGUE: LEGACIES

245 **His main source of income** "Agnew Keeps Low Profile as Maryland Businessman," *Boston Globe,* May 25, 1975.

245 **Agnew helped outfit** "Cameo Players in an '84 Deal with Iraq: Nixon, Agnew, Ceausescu," *New York Times,* June 1, 1990.

246 **short and urgent telegram** Agnew to Ahmed Abdul Wahab, telex, July 1980, private collection.

247 **The response was most welcome** Ahmed Abdul Wahab to Agnew, telex, July 14, 1980, private collection.

247 **Agnew claims in the letter** Agnew to His Royal Highness Prince Fahd bin Abdulaziz, draft of letter, Aug. 25, 1980, private collection.

249 **Agnew drafted a letter of thanks** Agnew to His Royal Highness Prince Fahd bin Abdulaziz, draft of letter, Sept. 16, 1980, private collection.

250 **He received a final letter back** His Royal Highness Prince Fahd bin Abdulaziz to Agnew, n.d., private collection.

250 **During a televised confrontation** Agnew, interview with Barbara Walters, *Today*, NBC, May 11, 1976.

251 **"Hating individual Jews"** William Safire, "Spiro Agnew and the Jews," *New York Times*, May 24, 1976.

251 **the architect of the Capitol** "Agnew's Head Absent from Lineup in Capitol," *Baltimore Sun*, April 8, 1991.

251 **"I am not blind or deaf"** Spiro T. Agnew, remarks at U.S. Senate bust unveiling, Washington, D.C., May 24, 1995.

252 **"I'm here to pay my respects"** "Guest List Covered Wide Spectrum," *Los Angeles Times*, April 28, 1994.

253 **"A life that might easily"** "A Little Help from His Friends," *Baltimore Sun*, Sept. 19, 1996.

253 **The black-and-white panel** Political cartoon by Paul Conrad, *Los Angeles Times*, Oct. 14, 1973.

254 **"Robert Dixon was a distinguished lawyer"** Walter E. Dellinger III, *The Rachel Maddow Show*, Feb. 21, 2019.

255 **Mueller cited the OLC policy** Special Counsel Robert S. Mueller III, "Report on the Investigation into Russian Interference in the 2016 Presidential Election," vol. 2, March 2019.

255 **"Under long-standing department policy"** Special Counsel Robert S. Mueller III, remarks to the press, Washington, D.C., May 29, 2019.

256 **"No one knows how many"** Commentary by David Brinkley, *NBC News Special Report,* Oct. 10, 1973.

260 **"I would hope first that"** Attorney General Elliot L. Richardson, remarks to the press, Washington, D.C., Oct. 11, 1973.

262 **"George Beall was a legendary"** "George Beall, U.S. Attorney for Maryland Who Prosecuted Agnew, Dies," *Baltimore Sun,* Jan. 17, 2017.

263 **"a very lonely time"** Profile of U.S. Attorney George Beall, *Baltimore Magazine,* Feb. 1974.

263 **"If I leave this office"** Associated Press, "Protege Probing Agnew," *Philadelphia Inquirer,* Aug. 9, 1973.

ABOUT THE AUTHORS

RACHEL MADDOW has hosted the Emmy Award–winning *Rachel Maddow Show* on MSNBC since 2008. She has a doctorate in politics from Oxford University and a bachelor's degree in public policy from Stanford University. She lives in Western Massachusetts with her partner, Susan Mikula, who—to this day—still wishes Maddow would get a proper teaching job.

MICHAEL YARVITZ is an Emmy and Peabody award–winning producer and journalist. He was the executive producer and co-writer of the podcast series *Bag Man*, which was the recipient of an Alfred I. duPont–Columbia University Award.